Michael Adams

Better Happy

D1457950

VIKING

Than Rich

**Canadians,
Money
and the
Meaning of Life**

VIKING

Published by the Penguin Group

Penguin Books Canada Ltd, 10 Alcorn Avenue, Toronto, Ontario, Canada M4V 3B2

Penguin Books Ltd, 27 Wrights Lane, London W8 5TZ, England

Penguin Putnam Inc., 375 Hudson Street, New York, New York 10014, U.S.A.

Penguin Books Australia Ltd, Ringwood, Victoria, Australia

Penguin Books (NZ) Ltd, cnr Rosedale and Airborne Roads, Albany, Auckland 1310, New Zealand

Penguin Books Ltd, Registered Offices: Harmondsworth, Middlesex, England

First published 2000

10 9 8 7 6 5 4 3 2 1

∞ Printed and bound in Canada on acid-free paper

Author representation: Westwood Creative Artists
94 Harbord Street, Toronto, Ontario M5G 1G6

CANADIAN CATALOGUING IN PUBLICATION DATA

Michael Adams, 1946 Sept. 29 –
Better happy than rich?: Canadians, money and the meaning of life

ISBN 0-670-88898-2

1. Wealth – Social Aspects – Canada. 2. Happiness.
3. Social values – Canada. I. Title.

Visit Penguin Canada's website at www.penguin.ca

For my parents,
William and Florentine Adams

Contents

Acknowledgments

No enterprise is more collaborative than survey research. Social researchers devise questions, random samples of respondents answer them, analysts torture the data till they tell the truth and lucky people like me take a shot at interpretation.

As with my first book, *Sex in the Snow*, I had a team of colleagues who helped me with this project:

- Sean Saraq brought his insight to the table and helped me create the template for this book. Although separated by very different demographics, Sean and I tend to see the world through the same socio-cultural prism.
- Amy Langstaff helped me put flesh on the analytical skeleton, suggesting the similes and metaphors that bring the data and concepts presented in this book to life.
- Dave Jamieson, our prince of multivariate analysis, together with his colleague Meytal Elhav, created the segmentation of our tribes that is the backbone of our socio-cultural work at Environics and the basis of this book.
- Sandra Sarner prepared the graphics and Erica Cerny pulled together the various drafts, each adding suggestions and insights along the way.
- Bruce Westwood, my agent, encouraged me as necessary and returned my tennis and verbal volleys with irritating regularity.
- Cynthia Good, my publisher, pushed me into regions of my imagination I would have ignored without her enthusiasm.

Throughout the project, the *Better Happy Than Rich?* team received both encouragement and intellectual support from our associates in the Environics group of companies: Environics' chairman, Derek Ruston, and our executive vice president, Barry Watson; Alain Giguère and his colleagues at CROP, who are also our partners in the Canadian 3SC program; Chris Baker, who heads our Ottawa office; Michael Heffring, Joan Bell and everyone else at Environics West; Bruce MacLellan and his co-workers at Environics Communications; and Doug Miller and his colleagues at Environics International.

To all of you, thanks. The errors, if any, should cause us all to be ashamed.

Introduction

It has been observed that authors often choose to write on subjects about which they wish to become more knowledgeable. They focus on things that intrigue them, and they hope that the process of writing a book will teach them something they did not know and help them to share their knowledge and insights with readers. Perhaps foremost among the author's hopes is that he will be able to instill in his readers a fascination with the topic of inquiry akin to his own.

A few years ago I wrote a book titled *Sex in the Snow*. My friends and colleagues know I am not an expert on either noun in that title. In fact, the subject of that book was the evolution of social values in Canada, and how the quest for autonomy, hedonism and spiritual meaning would define the mental posture of my fellow Canadians as we head into the new millennium.

When I admitted to those same friends and colleagues that I was now writing a book about money, they were even more sceptical about my expertise in this area. What do you know about money? You're a pollster! Isn't money a subject for economists, bankers, accountants or casino operators? I had to admit that when my publisher, Cynthia Good, first suggested I follow up *Sex in the Snow* with a book on money and its meaning in the lives of Canadians, I responded that I was interested in values, not money. "The guys on Bay Street have it all figured out anyway; it's about fear and greed, isn't it?" I joked.

Friends also chided me about the idea that I was writing one of those get-rich-quick self-help books that seem to dominate the shelves in every bookstore these days.

So let me say at the outset that reading this book may not immediately enrich your pocketbook, but I hope it will enrich your understanding of money and its meaning to Canadians. And if you are in the business of marketing to Canadian consumers, employing Canadian workers, gaining the trust of Canadian investors or encouraging the generosity of Canadian charitable donors, I hope you will find this book to be valuable in your work. If you have none of these practical applications in mind and are merely curious about yourself, people you know and your fellow Canadians, I hope you too will still find this book to be a helpful portrait of money and its changing meaning in our lives.

I claim no special expertise in the art of making, spending, saving, borrowing, investing or giving away money. In fact, I don't think I'm especially gifted in any of these departments. Only my kids think I'm a genius when it comes to money, and that's because I have never failed to produce the requisite forty-five cents when one of them has needed a Popsicle on a hot summer's day. Tennessee Williams's Blanche Dubois claimed to have "riches of the spirit"; my riches are the wonderful polling data Environics has accumulated over the decades, and the team of exceptional researchers expert in analyzing and interpreting those data for clients around the world.

In this book, I have chosen to focus the spotlight on Canadians' special orientation to money. What we do with money is telling: whether it's buying a forty-five-cent Popsicle that quenches thirst and momentarily bonds parent to child, purchasing a flashy sports car that impresses friends and strangers or depositing five dollars in the Salvation Army's plastic bubble two days before Christmas. I have chosen to write a book about money because what we do with our money is where the rubber really hits the road when it comes to expressing our values.

Money is a big subject—at times, I thought it was way too big for me or for one book. Still, I felt the readers of *Sex in the Snow*, as well as the thousands and thousands of Canadians who fill out our questionnaires each year, would be interested in the results of all our polling in this area.

I recall being very aware, as a small boy in Walkerton, Ontario, of money and the prestige it bought. In particular, I remember the day in 1955 when my dad brought home our brand-new, two-tone (coral and grey) Chevrolet Bel-Air convertible. Like any nine-year-old in the conformist 1950s, I knew that cars were status symbols, that money bought cars and that we were rich. Of course, the thrill wore off. I came to realize, after we left our small town and moved to the big city of Toronto, that we were not rich, just middle class like everybody else. As a teenager in the 1960s, I understood that any material comforts and status my family had achieved were the results of the full-time toil of both my parents. Dual-income households were much less common then; a working mother was a sign that a family was struggling just to be middle class. I knew that we were not poor, and that if I was a good student and worked hard I could get ahead in Canada. Even so, my friends and I would never have been able to go to university without student loans.

Like many Canadians I know, I claim to have little interest in money and the status symbols it can buy. These days, only the trendy Thrill-seeking Materialists in the youth cohort are unapologetically ostentatious consumers. And yet when I think of my own life, and see the attitudes and behaviours of my fellow Canadians as revealed in our surveys, I realize that money is probably the most important thing in our lives, next to our families. Money makes the world go round as never before: competition among ideologies and countries is being displaced by the competition among brands and the companies that own them.

There was a time not so long ago when money was important, but it wasn't everything. Religion was important; ethnicity was important; nationality was important; ancestry was important. And so was the afterlife that we assumed would follow death. Today, money is supplanting all these, and in so doing, it has achieved an unprecedented primacy as a lens through which we see ourselves and others. I argued in *Sex in the Snow* that our demographic characteristics— gender, age, ethno-cultural and social status—are declining in importance, and that our values are becoming more significant in explaining who we are and how our society is evolving. In this book I hope to show that instead of supplanting or eroding our values, money is becoming the primary manifestation of our values. The way Canadians earn, spend, invest and give away their money expresses how they think the world works—and how they would like to see it work. Understanding Canadians' social values is essential to understanding Canadians' financial behaviour and vice versa. In the pages to come, I hope to elucidate the relationship between these two intimately connected aspects of our lives.

A generation ago, the giant of twentieth-century literary criticism, Northrop Frye, observed, "Americans like to make money, Canadians like to audit it. I don't know of any other country where the accountant enjoys a higher social status." Today, as in many other aspects of Canadian life, Canadians see no distinction between our orientation to money and that of our American cousins. We assume that everybody wants to be a millionaire, and if you've got it, you flaunt it. But I think a closer examination of the two cultures reveals that while Canadians are just as fixated on money as Americans, we have very different attitudes about the symbolism of our expenditures and we are less willing to make personal sacrifices to realize our financial dreams. We are more willing than Americans to pay taxes to our governments in return for public services, which means they have a lot more discretionary income to play with. And our research at Environics has shown that we are much more prone to understatement than Americans when it comes to the ostentatious display of status symbols. We are less likely, as my granny used to say, to "put on airs."

It is instructive to compare the two societies in the way their popular cultures treat the subject of money these days. The hottest new quiz show in the U.S. is ABC's *Who Wants to Be a Millionaire?* Since its debut in 1999, the show has enjoyed huge ratings and has been emulated by other American networks with shows like *Greed* and *Twenty-One*. Over the past year, this format has been reproduced in twenty-one countries, and a one-time-only Canadian version of the popular show, hosted by journalist Pamela Wallin, will air in September 2000. With more than a hint of nationalist pride, the show's organizers have declared that the questions on the north-of-49° *Millionaire* will be more difficult than those posed by U.S. host Regis Philbin. But the less attractive purse (a full million, but in Canadian funds) and the fact that Wallin and company will merely be squatting on the American show's New York set are pointed reminders that Canadians are mere visitors in this cash-and-trivia land of Oz.

Although we may not be able to muster the funds (or the chutzpah?) necessary to launch a *Millionaire*-esque game show, as a culture we have certainly come a long way from the days when Gordon Sinclair, who played the role of curmudgeon on the CBC's *Front Page Challenge* for twenty-five years, bluntly asked guests, "How much money do you make?" In repeatedly advancing this simple but deliciously audacious query, Sinclair broke a huge taboo in Canadian society. The audience loved watching some beleaguered celebrity squirm as he or she attempted an awkward response. Even today, while mainstream magazines announce on their covers that their pages contain all manner of instruction in the pleasures of the flesh, and while our lust for real-life "dirt" brings us such invasive television fare as *Cops* and *Eyewitness Video*, the money taboo persists: fully one-fifth of Canadians admit that they would be upset if their friends knew how much money they earn, and one-quarter would be upset if their co-workers knew. Today's equivalents of Gordon Sinclair's pointed question are *Toronto Life*'s "Who Earns What?" issue and the annual publication of the salaries of the

CEOs of large public companies, the Canadian version of the Full Monty, when we get to see the fat wallets beneath those Armani suits.

Americans seem to be more comfortable with the nitty-gritty of the fiscal world so often seen as crass by Canadians. Perhaps because of the deeply ingrained ideology of vertical mobility and rugged individualism south of the border, Americans seem to have mythologized money more than Canadians have. In the U.S., money is part of a morality tale of rags to riches, of virtue rewarded. Americans associate money with all that is good, up to and including God: the phrase "In God we trust" is even imprinted on their currency. Witness also some titles appearing recently on American bookshelves: *Jesus CEO, The Management Methods of Jesus, Succeeding in Business Without Losing Your Faith, How to Get Rich . . . By the Book, The People Skills of Jesus.*

By contrast, Canadian bestsellers in recent years have included Peter Newman's *Titans*, the story of how "new money" is replacing "old money," and Rod McQueen's chronicle of the rise and fall of the Eatons, Canada's retail aristocracy. Unlike our American cousins, we do not admire the rich; we resent them. We cannot imagine how they got rich on the basis of hard work and merit alone; in our view, they must have known somebody or tricked many others.

A Canadian can almost forgive a multi-millionaire for his wealth if he drives a beaten-up Ford station wagon or has a reputation for frugality. Ken Thomson, our richest Canadian, is not a target for our resentment because his penchant for purchasing his ties only on deep-discount scratch-and-save "Bay Days" at a branch of the Hudson's Bay Company he once owned is legendary. But once a millionaire or one of his profligate children begins to display his wealth with a new Mercedes or other ostentatious symbols of excess, we know the dynasty is headed for disaster. We particularly resent inherited wealth, the quintessence of unearned good fortune. I know wealthy Torontonians who won't admit they live in Forest Hill or Rosedale, fearing the hatred they'd inspire.

They disguise their tony addresses by saying, "Just north of St. Clair" or "In the downtown area." They know they will not be admired for their wealth, and they don't want to be resented for it. In the U.S., you are made to feel guilty if you're poor. In Canada, this is also true to some extent. But north of the border, you are also made to feel guilty if you're rich. Only the middle class is beyond reproach.

You'd think there might be some Canadians who are seen to *earn* their high salaries: they play our de facto national sport for hockey teams in the U.S. or entertain us in the world of popular culture. However, three-quarters of Canadians disagree with the notion that professional athletes like Wayne Gretzky and entertainers like Celine Dion deserve the large amounts of money they are paid. While still admired on some level (perhaps "envied" is a better term), those who "make it" but forget that Canadians are staunch believers in understatement risk backlash. When Celine Dion renewed her marriage vows in an extravagant wedding feast in Las Vegas, even members of the Quebec media, usually slavishly admiring of their homegrown stars, described the event as "a tacky remake of *Aladdin.*"

At the top of the list of despised well-to-do Canadians is former prime minister Brian Mulroney. He seemed a little too American for most of us, and many Canadians were slightly hurt by the fact that he was the first prime minister in the nation's history for whom our highest political office seemed merely a stepping stone to something better in the world of corporate finance. Canadians have embraced instead the understated Jean Chrétien, who, millionaire though he is, tries to keep his head down and off the cover of *Frank* magazine, and in style is more Chevrolet than Porsche.

It should be noted, however, that despite our purported distaste for Americans' brash delight in money, we look to the south not without envy. The 1990s were rough for most Canadians. In terms of performance, it was the worst decade for the Canadian economy since the Second World War. Average annual gross domestic product growth in the 1990s was just 2.1 per cent—1 per cent less than the average pace in the 1980s, and more than three percentage points below 1960s levels. Our standard of living—what economists call real income—did not keep pace with inflation. Average Canadian family income after taxes was $43,300 in 1989, compared with $45,600 in 1997. Instead of climbing incomes, we have seen increasing taxes and user fees for public services that are eroding. In fact, the income tax burden rose steadily during the last decade, reaching an all-time high in 1999.

At the same time, our cousins to the south have enjoyed the most robust economic expansion in history, led by spectacular growth in the fields of new information, communications and biotechnologies. Family incomes in the U.S. are at record levels. Median household net worth grew from $60,900 in 1995 to $71,600 in 1998, an increase of 17.6 per cent (adjusted for inflation). In 1999, consumer spending rose at its fastest rate in ten years, and early in 2000 consumer confidence hit a new peak, breaking a record set in 1968.

Like children with our noses pressed against the candy-store window, we see the party to the south and wonder why we're not invited. Our purchasing power has declined from 78 per cent of that of the United States in 1978 to less than 66 per cent today. You have only to look at the value of our loonie to see what has happened to the status of ordinary Canadians compared with Americans. A devalued dollar invites foreign takeovers and lowers our standard of living. A dollar that's down 15 per cent has the effect of imposing a 15 per cent tariff on imports, and removing a 15 per cent tariff on exports. So rather than increase our productivity to compete with the U.S. economy, we have simply slashed the prices of the goods we produce by slashing the value of our currency. In this way, we've also increased the price we pay for American goods. No wonder we find ourselves resentfully expressing distaste for the States.

We saw fascinating evidence of the Canadian culture of resentment within our own borders with the entrepreneur

Gerry Schwartz's ill-fated takeover bid for Canadian Airlines and Air Canada in 1999. At first, Canadians were intrigued by Schwartz's bold move; he even charmed the Canadian Auto Workers' union chief, Buzz Hargrove, into supporting his plan. In the end, however, he was bested by Air Canada's American CEO, Robert Milton, not only in the courts but also in the arena of public opinion. Canadians became less enamoured of Schwartz as they learned more about his lavish lifestyle than they cared to know: everything from cottages in Nantucket to homes in Bermuda and Florida to tony breakfasts with his equally posh wife, Heather Reisman, in their Rosedale mansion. It was all a bit much, and in the end Canadians were relieved that this all-too-successful Canadian entrepreneur and friend of the prime minister lost out to the less-colourful management of our putative national airline. Robert Milton and his advisers had learned from former Bank of Montreal CEO Matthew Barrett that Canadians do not want their corporate captains to be celebrities; "ordinary folk" want the giants to remain anonymous, so as not to be reminded of their own relative poverty and insignificance.

It is no accident that it was in Canada that the shareholder-activist Yves Michaud put forth his proposals for corporate reform. At the 1998 Canadian Imperial Bank of Commerce annual meeting, Michaud's proposals—which included suggestions that top executive pay be limited to twenty times the average pay in the bank, that board members be voted on individually rather than as a slate and that executives not receive cut-rate loans—received surprisingly strong backing. In the U.S., these proposals likely would have been seen as preposterous. Here, they actually received a hearing, and even some shareholder support.

Part of the disparity between Canadians' and Americans' behaviour towards money may stem from the stark differences in the degree of control citizens of these two countries have over the money they earn. Even though most Canadians believe in the social contract and have a strong desire not to become like our neighbours to the south in terms of public policy, there is an undercurrent of resentment in Canada over the fact that we have to pay for this privilege.

More than half of Canadians resent the rich, but one-fifth of us also admit to resenting the poor, and to feeling that people who meet with misfortune have brought it on themselves. The cynical Canadian consciousness has conjured countless stereotypes of the undeserving poor: welfare cheats, illegal immigrants with fraudulent health cards, whole regions of the country living the life of Riley on employment insurance benefits, fishermen being paid not to fish and farmers being paid not to grow things. Our research has shown that almost all Canadians, regardless of income, describe themselves as "middle class." Not surprisingly, the middle class has become a sanctimonious safe haven from the iniquity of poverty or wealth. Unlike the other two economic categories, the middle class, in the minds of Canadians, can do no wrong.

Our private attitudes about money are also reflected in Canadian public policy and in our national preoccupation with fiscal formulae to equalize "have" and "have-not" provinces. Of all the polls I have seen on Canadians' attitudes towards their country, I have found the most telling to be one showing that the citizens in each and every province believe that their province sends more money to Ottawa than it receives back in the form of transfers and services. Every province, including Newfoundland and Quebec, has this notion bred in the bone. We have built a nation not only on the basis of "peace, order and good government," but also on uniting from sea to sea those whose relationship to government is one of resentful dependence.

According to Statistics Canada, from 1975 to 1996, our governments ran their spending up to an annual average of 49 per cent of GDP, but taxed us only 44 of those percentage points. Two-thirds of the extra taxes we now pay are devoted to paying not for today's programs but for what we consumed yesterday.

This frustrating backlog in payments accounts for the strong current of resentment against "the system." Canadians are more focused on immediate gratification than ever, but they are forced to pay up to a quarter of their taxes not for current consumption, which they want, or for tomorrow's consumption, which they hope for, but for yesterday's consumption, which they would rather forget.

So while politicians congratulate themselves on balancing the books, average Canadians do not see much of a dividend for our new fiscal rectitude. In fact, no sooner have we declared victory over deficits than economists tell us our economic growth is sluggish (Canada was twenty-fourth out of twenty-five OECD countries in growth of real GDP per capita from 1988 to 1998), and the same business leaders who encouraged us to embrace free trade with the U.S. are now warning Canadians that we are losing control of our industries to American ownership. In 1999 alone, as of November 30, Americans had gobbled up $25.6 billion worth of Canadian companies, including the symbolically important Eaton's department store chain, which was absorbed by its U.S. rival, Sears.

How are our national and personal finances affecting our world-views? In *Sex in the Snow*, I described our evolution since the 1950s from a shy, unemotional and unassuming people—deferential to traditional institutional authority, delaying pleasure to later in life (or even until the afterlife)—to a more autonomous, hedonistic and self-confident nation. Our spirituality began to be expressed in thousands of personal ways, rather than through conformity to traditional religious practice and belief. Comforted by our traditions of civility, compromise and the pragmatic blending of liberalism, toryism and socialism, we found ourselves able to question, then reject, the power of traditional hierarchies, patriarchy, sexism and racism. I saw us evolving into a "postmodern" society with flexible personalities, identities and communities. It was an optimistic story, and one I believe could still come true. However, hard on the heels of my book's publication, numerous socio-cultural signs began to suggest that the spirit and optimism of Canadians had been broken, or at least severely compromised.

Despite having an economy that appears to have turned the corner, Canadians feel less confident in their ability to adapt successfully to complexity and change. Before 1997, these were more often seen as challenges we would meet on our personal road to self-fulfillment. Now, change and complexity seem like hurdles put in place by corporate leaders, who appear to be the main beneficiaries of our increased labour and stress. There is a strong sense that the middle class is disappearing (despite the fact that most Canadians see themselves as members), and record levels of personal debt remind us that if we stop working, even for a short period of time, we and our families may fall through one of the many holes in our social safety net, into the lower class or worse.

Some of the fear that Canadians have felt as their confidence has diminished has translated into a desire for strong leadership. Although the overall trend in Canadian society is still towards increased autonomy, leaders such as Mike Harris in Ontario and Ralph Klein in Alberta speak to a desire among many Canadians for simplicity, order and direction. It is not Canadians with the most modern values who have put Harris in power and kept him there; it is those with more traditional values who are facing an uncertain world and trying to cling to a system in which they can feel more secure.

Some people, following the example of the demographer David Foot, will suggest that the growing search for security and stability over the past few years is a natural result of an aging population. However, the fact is that the Canadian population was aging long before this trend towards stability appeared; until 1997, values were modernizing, focusing more on personal autonomy and experience-seeking than on traditional ideals of security and stability. Demography is only one factor in social change, and it certainly is not our destiny. What, then, is driving the change in mood?

Many Canadians believe that in recent years, our governments and corporations have been doing well, but that individual Canadians have not. Ordinary people feel the system is working not for them but for a financial elite. And there is a growing popular reaction against this *nomenklatura*, as expressed by events such as the WTO protests in Seattle and the release of bestsellers such as Naomi Klein's *No Logo: Taking Aim at the Brand Bullies*, movies such as *Fight Club* and albums such as Rage Against the Machine's *Battle of Los Angeles.*

At one time, Canadians felt that they had power as citizens—one person, one vote. Now they feel that what little power they have is as consumers—one dollar, one vote. Perhaps not surprisingly, the growing psychographic diversity I described in *Sex in the Snow* is increasingly influenced by a prevailing climate of insecurity and aimlessness. Nonetheless, a fundamental shift to autonomy, hedonism and a personal definition of spirituality still holds, and it remains to be seen whether Canadians will regain their sense of adaptability and vitality in the first few years of the new millennium. Clearly, their orientation towards money will be key.

It became evident through our research that the meanings people ascribe to money are as diverse as the Canadian population itself—for some, money means security and stability; for others it means freedom, and for others still, fun and experience-seeking. Some more materialistic Canadians like money not only for the status it conveys, but also simply for the joy of just having it, an attitude condemned by John M. Keynes in his *Essays in Persuasion*:

> The love of money as a possession—as distinguished from the love of money as a means to the enjoyments and realities of life—will be recognized for what it is, a somewhat disgusting morbidity, one of those semi-criminal, semi-pathological propensities which one hands over with a shudder to the specialists in mental disease.

Though he was not Canadian, Keynes sums up a dominant strain in Canadian thought. Given our love/hate relationship with cold, hard cash, and money's status as an integral component of our lives and our world-views, I thought it appropriate that the sequel to *Sex in the Snow* should be titled *Better*

Happy Than Rich?: Canadians, Money and the Meaning of Life. The question mark in the title is appropriate not only for a pollster who poses questions for a living but for a people who are profoundly ambivalent about money and its growing importance in their lives.

1.

Social Change in Canada

Have you ever been on a subway or bus in one of our major cities and found yourself sizing up the other passengers, wondering who they are, where they have come from, where they are going and what they're thinking? Pollsters cannot help being curious about other people. We wonder about the teenage boy with spiked yellow hair, baggy pants and the Stone Cold Steve Austin T-shirt. We wonder about the two slightly older girls, one of Chinese descent, the other perhaps with parents or grandparents from Portugal or Italy, on their way to college with their backpacks filled with school-related stuff, pagers, cellphones and teen magazines. The woman in her thirties with the child in a designer walker: mother or nanny? The serious man buried in the *Report on Business*: was he born with a suit on? The middle-aged guy balding on top but with a ponytail at the back: was he at the original Woodstock? What about Woodstock '99?

Besides the fact that Canada has become a multicultural salad, and that a lot of people look unique and dress in their own individual style, the few moments we spend on the subway don't tell us much about these strangers. They do remind us that the people we spend most of our lives with, our friends and families, are usually much like us, but that the rest of the world is composed of a bewildering variety of people. Their faces, their clothes, the way they walk and the snippets we overhear of their conversations give us only superficial clues to the real people inside.

In the past, we could assume that demography was destiny. If we knew someone's gender, age, education and income, we knew pretty well everything that mattered about the person. Stereotypes were usually pretty close to the mark. We all went through the same life-cycle changes (such as adolescence, childbirth and death) at about the same time, and certainly in the same order as everyone else. We also enjoyed the same rituals and rites of passage as everyone else. Those who didn't conform were labelled eccentrics or worse, and were relegated to the periphery of mainstream society. They weren't allowed into the club, if they even bothered to apply.

Today, the ties that bind us to, or divide us from, others are not our shared demographics but rather our values. The values consensus that ruled Canada in the 1950s has fragmented. We are not all motivated by the same set of Judeo-Christian social norms as we were fifty years ago. Yet on another level, we are now united by a growing tolerance for ethnic and cultural diversity that was not evident then. This tolerance for difference is probably Canada's most admirable contribution to global civilization. It distinguishes this country from Europe, where political parties whose platforms and rhetoric revolve around combating the loss of ethnic and racial "purity" enjoy considerable electoral support, and it distinguishes us from the United States, where ethnicity and race continue to be the bases of deep division.

The growing diversity of social values "tribes" (which I discussed in *Sex in the Snow* and which Environics continues to measure and track), when seen in the larger context of the issue of tolerance, explains much of what is unique about us: how we can see the growth of personal autonomy, hedonistic pleasure and a personal definition of spirituality, even as we retain a strong commitment to the fundamental tenets of Canadian civil society.

Our American cousins began their republic with a Declaration of Independence in 1776 that dedicated that nation to "life, liberty and the pursuit of happiness." More than a century later, when Canadians reluctantly began their own nation with the British North America Act in 1867, our version of Thomas Jefferson's ringing declaration was "peace, order and good government." As we enter the third millennium, can we say that modern citizens of these two countries have achieved the ideals set out by their founding forebears? Well, to quote another great American, the rock star Meatloaf,

"Two out of three ain't bad." The Americans have life and liberty, and we have peace and order. Each of us is still working
on happiness and good government.

The word "sex" in the title of my first book signified the
new values that have evolved in Canadian culture, but that
have not completely melted the "snow" of our traditional values, which to some extent persist and continue to differentiate
us from Americans. In fact, I devoted an entire chapter of *Sex
in the Snow* to differences in the values of Canadians and
Americans, some of which are dramatic and have significant
manifestations in the everyday lives of average citizens.

Environics has been systematically tracking the evolution
of social values in the United States for the past decade. This
research has allowed us to see how the growing globalization
of commerce, culture and communications is causing the values of Canadians to further merge with or diverge from those
of Americans. Americans don't care much about this phenomenon, but Canadians do, and these sorts of findings are
relevant not only to key issues in Canadian public policy but
also to the world of consumer marketing. The beer company
Molson brought back its "I am Canadian" campaign because
of its spectacular success in appealing to the not-always-
understated Canadian sense of national pride.

Since writing *Sex in the Snow*, I have done hundreds of
presentations of the material in that text. Like my friend David
Foot, the author of the monumental bestseller *Boom, Bust and
Echo*, I have become a talking book. In these presentations, I
describe not only how we have changed as a people but also
how we have divided ourselves into social values tribes and
how our values compare with those of Americans.

The research we at Environics conduct in this country and
around the world enables us to place the evolution of
Canadian social values in a global context. We find that
Canada's socio-cultural development has been proceeding
according to a pattern described by the academics Neil
Nevitte and Ron Inglehart in their *World Values Study*.
Canadians, like many others around the world, are moving

along a trajectory that begins with traditional deference to institutional authority, moves through the achievement motivation and conspicuous consumption of modernity, and then proceeds towards the quest for harmony, well-being and spiritual meaning characteristic of postmodernity.

Traditional, Modern and Postmodern Society			
Societal Goals and Individual Values			
	Traditional	*Modern*	*Postmodern*
Core Societal Project	Survival in a steady-state economy	Maximize economic growth	Maximize subjective well-being
Individual Value	Traditional religious and communal norms	Achievement motivation	Post-materialist and postmodern values
Authority System	Traditional authority	Rational-legal authority	De-emphasis of both legal and religious authority

Source: Ronald Inglehart. Modernization and Post-modernization

We began our own Canadian surveys in 1983, and now we have accumulated a total of more than forty-five thousand interviews with representative samples of Canadians, tracking the evolution of social values in this country. Only France, Italy and the United States have archives of social values research as extensive as our own. Our surveys have been probing social change annually for almost two decades, using a battery of approximately 250 questions to track about one hundred social values, trends, motivations and socio-cultural characteristics. Computer analyses of the responses enable us to construct a "map" of our socio-cultural values. (For a more complete explanation of how our 3SC social values map is constructed, please see Appendix B.)

At the top of the map are people who conform to traditional values of order, authority, discipline and the Judeo-Christian moral code. In essence, these values suggest that there are

The Axes of Social Change

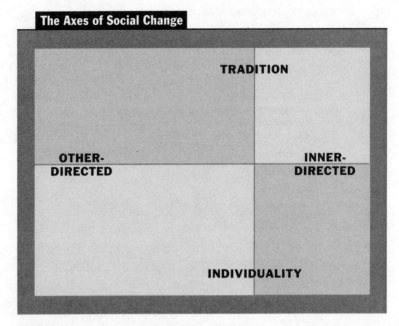

TRADITION

OTHER-
DIRECTED

INNER-
DIRECTED

INDIVIDUALITY

routines, rituals and rules of conduct in our society, and that these norms must be abided by in all circumstances. At the bottom of the map are those who question and often reject traditional values. They do not automatically defer to religious, patriarchal or hierarchical authority. The people at the top of the map stop at Stop signs even if no one is going through the intersection; the people at the bottom see Stop signs as non-binding recommendations.

At the left of the socio-cultural map are those who are socially inclined or other-directed. They are more expressive and outgoing. The more traditional ones do everything they can—say the right things, wear the right clothes, admire the right icons—to gain the approval of their peers and reference groups and avoid their disapproval. The more modern ones are very focused on others but are less image-driven.

At the right-hand side of the map are the inner-directed in our society. They do not care what anyone thinks about the opinions they express, the clothes they wear or the party they vote for. They do their own thing. The more traditional ones

Position of Selected Trends on the Socio-Cultural Map

TRADITION		

OTHER-DIRECTED

Ostentatious Consumption

Primacy of the Family

Religiosity

Confidence in Government

Need for Status Recognition

Financial Concern for the Future

Anomie   Risk-aversion

Hyper-rationality

Social Darwinism

INNER-DIRECTED

Enthusiasm for Technology

Flexibility of Personality

Personal Creativity

Flexibility of Gender Identity

Adaptability to Complexity in Life

Heterarchy

Need for Autonomy

Rejection of Order

Control of Destiny

Rejection of Authority

INDIVIDUALITY

tend to imagine that they are always right; the more modern ones are more inclined to think that everyone has a right to his or her own opinion.

A method we call factor analysis of correspondence places the values on the socio-cultural map. In the upper-right-hand quadrant, we see the values of people who venerate tradition and are inner-directed. They are strong on values such as financial concern for the future, risk-aversion, hyper-rationality (suppress, don't show, your emotions), social Darwinism (it's a dog-eat-dog world, and there is nothing we can do about it) and anomie (a sense of disconnectedness from the socio-cultural changes taking place in the wider society). These people believe that things have gone downhill in our society since the Sunday evening in 1956 when Ed Sullivan welcomed Elvis Presley to his show. If you had to label the mental posture of the people in this quadrant, it would be Financial Independence, Stability and Security.

In the upper-left-hand quadrant are the values of people who adhere to tradition and are social or other-directed. They

The Socio-Cultural Map

TRADITION

OTHER-DIRECTED		INNER-DIRECTED
Traditional Communities, Institutions and Social Status		Financial Independence, Stability and Security
Experience-seeking and New Frontiers		Personal Control and Self-fulfillment

INDIVIDUALITY

are strong on religiosity, primacy of the family and confidence in government, and they have a need for status recognition, which is displayed through their ostentatious consumption of symbolically resonant goods and services. People in this quadrant look to institutions to provide cradle-to-grave security in this life and everlasting solace in the next. These people believe in a hierarchy of leaders and followers, and in climbing the ladder of social success. Start with a Ford or a Chevy, move up to a Buick or an Olds, and dream of someday owning a Lincoln or a Caddie. Everything you own or buy is a symbol of your position in the social hierarchy. The mental posture of people in this quadrant can be described as an orientation towards Traditional Communities, Institutions and Social Status.

In the lower-right-hand quadrant are inner-directed people who are individualistic in orientation. They are strong on values like rejection of authority, control of destiny (we control our fate, not the stars in the sky or who our father happened to be), need for autonomy and rejection of order (the idea that there is a place for everything and everything in its place).

The latter trait, together with their embrace of heterarchy (the belief that leadership structures should be fluid and responsive to change, not static hierarchies), shows a desire to dress and act informally, and to allow for flexible models of leadership rather than adhere to a structured hierarchy. These people value equality, spontaneity and authenticity. They reject titles, uniforms and routine, and they create their own rituals. The mental posture of the people in this quadrant can be summed up as Personal Control and Self-fulfillment.

In the lower-left-hand quadrant, we find people who reject traditional authority but are other-directed. They are strong on values like adaptability to complexity in life, adaptive navigation (change is an opportunity, not a threat), personal creativity, plus two other postmodern values: flexibility of personality and flexibility of gender identity (the appropriation of personality traits and identities usually associated with the opposite sex, with younger people, with other cultures). These people also have an enthusiasm for technology because it allows them to transcend traditional roles, institutions and boundaries, and to connect virtually with communities of people with similar values, interests and lifestyles around the world. These are the people who often spend a lot of time online. The mental posture that sums up their orientation is Experience-seeking and New (Mental) Frontiers.

When we at Environics first began this social values research, the average Canadian was located in the upper-left quadrant, the one associated with Traditional Communities, Institutions and Social Status. During the past two decades, however, Canadians have been gradually moving down and to the right of the map—that is, away from traditional values towards more modern ones, and away from other-direction towards inner-direction. In 1983, 25 per cent of us were in the lower third of the map. By 1999, it was 38 per cent, representing something just under a 1 per cent shift each year: not the kind of cataclysmic shifts in public opinion newspapers love to report, but in our view, a much more important and significant evolution of value currents in our society and culture.

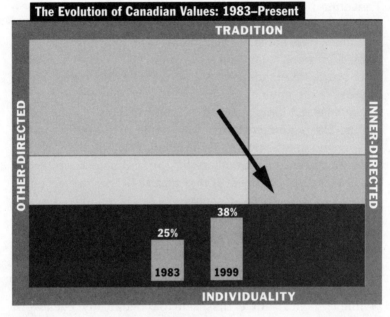

The Evolution of Canadian Values: 1983–Present

TRADITION

OTHER-DIRECTED

INNER-DIRECTED

38%

25%

1983   1999

INDIVIDUALITY

There is no single explanation for the overall direction of socio-cultural change in Canada. The factors that influence our culture are numerous. The ubiquity of mass media, to which has been added the interactivity of the Internet; our economy's increasing integration with that of the United States and other countries; the change in the ethno-cultural composition of our country; our increasing levels of formal education—all have played some part in the change I have just described. Add to these ingredients the fact that every year two groups—a new batch of fifteen-year-olds and a new group of immigrants—are polled for the first time even as another group of older Canadians shuffles off this mortal coil (taking their values with them to that great random sample in the sky), and you have a recipe for profound and lasting social change.

A few years ago, I asked our computer wizards to do a sys-tematic analysis of the questions,that are used to create our socio-cultural map. I wanted to see which items had been moving in the same direction since 1983, and which I could use to illustrate the fundamental currents of social change in our culture. There are about ten items that do this, but one stands out in my mind as being particularly important. It is the response to the statement of a traditional value: "The father of the family must be the master in his own house." In 1983, when we first measured this, 42 per cent of Canadians strongly or somewhat agreed with this statement. Nearly every year since then, the proportion of Canadians in agreement has declined. By 1999 it was only 19 per cent.

Very few trends move in one direction so systematically. The decline in patriarchal authority is one of the most significant currents of social change in our culture. It both reflects and effects changes in the roles and status of fathers, mothers and children in the family; it has implications for patriarchal and hierarchical authority in the workplace; it has implications for the candidates considered for leadership positions in our governments, businesses and voluntary organizations. And in my view, this decline in patriarchal authority is a natural by-product of our earlier movement away from deference to traditional religious authority. After we dismissed the priests, rabbis and ministers, questioning Dad was easy.

There are some demographic differences in Canadians' responses to this statement.

Father Must Be Master in His Own House

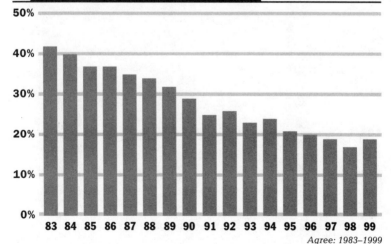

Agree: 1983–1999

Twenty-five per cent of men agree that the father must be the master in his own house (which means, of course, that three-quarters of Canadian men disagree with this traditional rule), compared with 13 per cent of women. Only 15 per cent of those with college or university education agree with this traditional value, but 29 per cent of those in the blue-collar occupations do. The most significant differences in attitudes regarding automatic patriarchal authority are generational, as the chart below plainly illustrates.

It appears that the Baby Boomers are the generation that represents the big break with the traditional value of deference to patriarchal authority, although it may be that the Elders are the true revolutionaries when it comes to questioning patriarchy. After all, the parents of the Baby Boomers deliberately decided, in their millions, to raise their children according to the wisdom of Dr. Benjamin Spock rather than that of their own folks. Subsequently, the Boomers embraced this new egalitarianism in numbers never before seen, making it a cornerstone of their ideology. Today it would appear

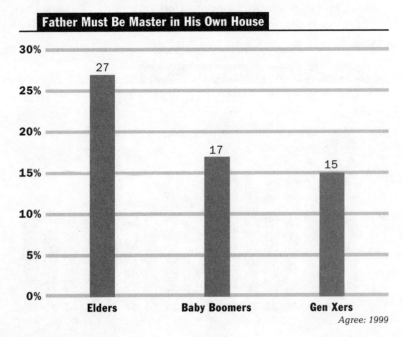

Father Must Be Master in His Own House

Agree: 1999

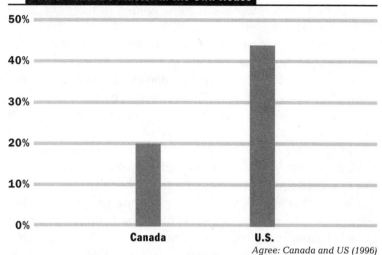

Father Must Be Master in His Own House

Agree: Canada and US (1996)

that, *pace* David Frum and Danielle Crittenden, Gen Xers have not "come to their senses," but rather continue to embrace the ideal of egalitarianism they have inherited from their progressive parents.

Those who think our integration into American culture is inevitable, given the torrent of U.S. music, movies and television programs in our lives, should compare the responses in Canada with those in the U.S. on this item. More than twice as many Americans (44 per cent) think that the father knows best. This is a remarkable finding, and one that has significant implications for the structure of authority not only in families, but also in organizations like the workplace and those in civil society.

A few months ago, I was with four close friends on a golfing getaway. Somehow, we started talking about our fathers. It turned out to be a surprisingly emotional topic among guys for whom the suppression of emotion on and off the golf course is an implicit virtue. I had the singular good fortune of being the only son who did not hate his father. Each of these men had committed himself to being to his own son the father he had never had. It is interesting to note that among the group on the trip, I was the only Canadian citizen and the only Baby Boomer; the others all belonged to the generation that preceded my own.

Of course, my golfing companions are not the only men who want to be better fathers to their children. Have you noticed the tendency of Canadian dads these days to address their little boys as "buddy"? What could better express the earnest quest of the Canadian male not to be a traditional father to his son but to be his equal and his friend? Buddy. It is as sweet as it is Canadian. Will it still be Buddy if he turns out to be gay or marries a girl of another race? Maybe, maybe not. But in Canada, odds are the answer will be yes.

The "father knows best" example is but one of many that show that some of our "eternal verities" have turned out to be not so eternal. Just a couple of generations ago, the belief that the father of the family must be master in his house was entrenched in our culture, as entrenched as it had been since the days of Adam and Eve. Today, fewer than two in ten Canadians agree. When we examine striking data such as these, we begin to realize that another eternal truth no longer holds: *Plus ça change, plus c'est la même chose*—the more things change, the more they stay the same. As I have shown, things do change, some really important things, including our fundamental values.

Demographics too are changing. While everlasting life is still not possible, we have increased the average lifespan by almost 50 per cent in the twentieth century, from fifty-five years in 1900 to seventy-six years in 2000. That fact alone makes us think differently about life and its possibilities. There is not such a rush to get into the workforce when you know you'll live till seventy-six. And there's certainly no need to feel old at thirty.

Fertility rates (the number of children conceived by the average woman) have declined in this century from 3.8 in 1900 to 1.7 in 2000. Were it not for the two hundred thousand or so immigrants we typically attract to Canada each year, our population would be in decline.

And there's more change in the offing—not just because new technologies will be invented, as surely they will, or because of the globalization of commerce, culture and communications, but also because new values are emerging in our culture, in part owing to the growing diversity of what we at Environics call social values tribes.

When we place the members of the three generations on our map, the average Elder is in the upper half of the map, right between the upper two quadrants with their traditional values. My peers in the Baby Boomer generation are in the lower right "personal autonomy" quadrant and Gen Xers are in the experience-seeking ("sex, drugs and rap") quadrant. Right where you would expect them to be.

But while averages tell a truth, they also disguise more precise truths. A segmentation analysis of each of these generational groups reveals significant clusters, or "tribes," within each generation, and it is the awareness and understanding of these tribes that will differentiate the astute marketer and human-resource manager of the future from

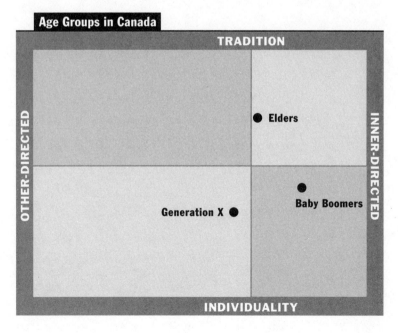

those who insist on using strategies based on stereotypes that are going to be increasingly off the mark as time marches on. In the future, the most successful marketing, business and political strategists will recognize the existence not only of different demographic characteristics in our society but also of different social values tribes.

2.

Canada's Thirteen Social Values Tribes

In *Sex in the Snow*, I described three different gener-ations of Canadians—Elders (pre-Boomers); Baby Boomers (the cohort born between 1946 and 1964) and Gen Xers (post-Boomers). Elders tend to conform to traditional values, Boomers are more autonomous and Gen Xers generally seek novelty and experience. However, one of the main aims of my first book was to point out that these generations are far from homogeneous in their social values. We do not necessarily behave in prescribed ways at various ages, nor do people of the same age respond in exactly the same way to externalities like economic cycles, new technology or political events.

Demography is destiny in the sense that we tend to do certain things (leave school, get married, retire, die) in age ranges that demographers can predict. But those ranges are getting wider and wider as time goes on, and with the exception of death, these and other life-cycle events are becoming less likely to occur in the same order. The past fifty years of our history have witnessed more and more exceptions to our cultural norms; "exceptions" have become so commonplace that what were once thought to be norms have themselves become exceptions. For example, the traditional nuclear family (a wage-earning dad, a stay-at-home mom and 2.5 children born when the mother was in her twenties) has evolved from the cultural norm of the 1950s to the exceptional minority of the 1990s. Why? Values have changed, and not least among the changes in our values has been our radically altered perception of the role and status of women in our society.

As we observe changes in social values, it is sometimes tempting to discuss various generations of Canadians as homogeneous groups. After all, don't young people do and think new things while old people do and think old things? In some cases, yes. And certainly, generalizations made on the basis of age have some truth to them. But in light of the diversity of Canadians in the Elder, Boomer and Gen X cohorts, it is very dangerous to put any serious money behind dated stereotypes of Granddad and Junior. This danger becomes particularly grave in the case of Gen Xers, who are more diverse than any previous generation of Canadians. Sophisticated consumer marketers have become well aware of the growing diversity of North American youth tribes in the 1990s, and others who persist in ignoring the marked variations among these young people do so at their peril. Before we examine Canada's youth tribes, and those in the older generations, allow me to offer a few words on methodology.

In our social values research, the values and attitudes of Canadians are plotted on the socio-cultural map that was introduced in the last chapter. This map shows not only how strong or weak Canadians are on certain values compared with the overall Canadian average but also how specific values are conceptualized (and contextualized) by displaying them in close proximity to other associated values.

The construction of the socio-cultural map is a multi-stage statistical process that uses as its raw material the 2,600 interviews with Canadians we conduct annually using our 3SC Social Values Monitor. As the years go by and new values and motivations are identified through focus groups, one-on-one interviews or simple social observation, we add questions to our survey.

Our 2,600 Canadian respondents are asked about 250 questions regarding their fundamental motivations and attitudes, as well as hundreds of additional questions about their personal characteristics and lifestyles, the brands they admire and the products they use. The individual questions are analyzed and grouped into about one hundred values (or trends). The trends are then placed on the socio-cultural map using factor analysis of correspondence. In this way, trends appear on the map in close proximity to the values with which they are most highly correlated. For example, values such as rejection of authority, control of destiny, equality of the sexes, and pursuit of happiness to the detriment of duty correlate with one another: together they indicate a mental posture, or overall way of looking at the world, through a lens of personal autonomy, control and self-fulfillment. Therefore, these values all appear in the same area of the 3SC map (the lower-right-hand quadrant). Similar clusterings take place in the case of "traditional" values and "experience-seeking" values.

As we saw in the last chapter, trends appearing near the top of the map are correlated with a world-view that conforms to tradition. Those at the bottom reflect a more modern (or even postmodern) perspective, one that questions, and often rejects, traditional values. Trends on the left side of the map correspond to a more social, expressive and other-directed approach to life that attaches a great deal of importance to others and the opinions of others. Those on the right side reflect a more inner-directed perspective.

Values in the upper-left "Traditional Other-Directed" quadrant for the most part relate to a desire for social status and success, and indicate faith in traditional communities like one's family and ethnic group, and institutions like the church and government. Also found in this quadrant are people who are very comfortable with the status quo or even, among the Elders, the status quo ante (that is, before the 1960s). These people trust the judgment of others and are the most likely to defer to the wisdom of their elders, their church, government, business leaders and professional elites like doctors and lawyers. This is where you find people who want nothing so much as to fit into the crowd. Interestingly, it is also where you find the people who are focused on "standing out from the crowd," but always in a way that will impress others. They want to stand out from the crowd *within* the crowd, to be admired. Among older people in this quadrant, the goal is keeping up with the Joneses; among younger, it's a carefully displayed knowledge of brand names and labels, sports heroes and popular cultural icons.

Moving over to the upper-right "Traditional Inner-Directed" quadrant, we find trends that tend to relate to a focus on security and stability in all areas of life, from one's home life to one's finances. These people want to be independent, to stand on their own two feet and to know that they will be safe regardless of what happens. Among Elders, this desire for independence is manifested in a concern for security in old age; among young people, it is expressed in a desire for a good job, a reliable spouse and a secure foundation in life. People in this quadrant are not at all comfortable with the long-term direction of social change in Canada, or with the political priorities of our central government. In Quebec, they tend to vote for the Bloc Québécois and in the rest of Canada for Reform and its successor coalition.

In the lower-right "Modern Inner-Directed" quadrant are values having to do with freedom and personal fulfillment. The trends in this quadrant reflect scepticism of the status quo and a rejection of the values in the upper-left quadrant—deference to authority, participation in traditional institutions and other-directed consumerism. This quadrant is where you find people who "do their own thing." They don't try to fit in, but they don't try to stand out either. They have no interest in joining the club but, if so inclined, will start their own. They are the most independent-minded of Canadians, and for that reason they are among the most difficult to stereotype. They range from the entrepreneurial mavericks who made JDS Uniphase and PMC Sierra into multi-billion-dollar New Economy rockets to the brilliant and idealistic CBC producer Mark Starowicz, who gave us some of the best public-affairs programming Canada has ever seen, including "The Journal" and the CBC series on the history of television.

Finally, the values in the lower-left "Modern Other-Directed" quadrant are generally leading edge and can be described as postmodern. They reflect an adaptability to change and complexity, an openness to (and even craving for) everything that is new. A certain hedonism resides in this quadrant—not the status-seeking, materialistic hedonism of the upper-left quadrant, but rather an experiential version. These people wish to push the envelope of what it is to be human and to experience life with emotional intensity. They have a great interest in communities—though not traditional communities of family, religion, ethnicity and nationality found in the upper-left quadrant. They prefer communities of choice: networks of kindred spirits and global connections, often made on the Internet or through travel.

If the "average Canadian" were placed on the map, he or she would be found at the intersection of the two axes. This mythical average Canadian would have some interest in traditional communities, institutions and social status but would also value personal autonomy and self-fulfillment. He or she would desire financial independence, security and stability but would also exhibit some interest in experience-seeking and new communities. Needless to say, this average Canadian doesn't exist in the flesh.

One of the most important lessons I've learned in three decades of polling is that averages and generalizations about large populations almost always conceal significant differ-

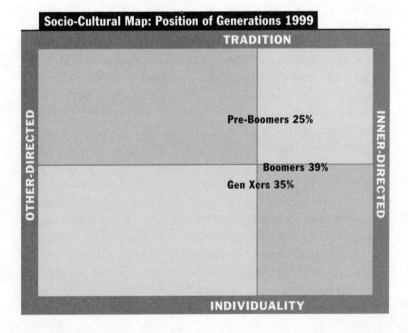

Socio-Cultural Map: Position of Generations 1999

TRADITION

OTHER-DIRECTED

INNER-DIRECTED

Pre-Boomers 25%

Boomers 39%
Gen Xers 35%

INDIVIDUALITY

ences. There are moments when we think and act in the same way, but those moments, such as our collective reaction to Paul Henderson's legendary goal in the 1972 Canada–Russia hockey series, are very rare indeed. This is why there's a need for a more extensive, segmented analysis of the three generations of Canadians and of the distinct social values tribes in each age group.

The Elders—25 Per Cent of Canadian Population

Key Values	
Strong on	*Weak on*
risk-aversion	enthusiasm for consumption
religiosity	flexible definition of family
everyday ethics	penchant for risk-taking
community involvement	neo-romanticism
legacy	sexual permissiveness

Born before the end of the Second World War, the Elders have seen more than their fair share of gut-wrenching instability, most notably depression and war. These experiences are the main reasons they are so motivated by security and stability; they know from first-hand experience that the bottom can fall out of the economy, and they sense that there are plenty of bad people in this world, even in this country, who pose a personal threat to them and to civil society. Indeed, for the Elders, security and stability are almost universal values in the sense that few are able to focus on personal autonomy and self-fulfillment, or on experiential values, unless they have first achieved a certain degree of stability.

Thus it is perhaps not surprising that the value that best characterizes the eldest Elders overall is *risk-aversion*. They do not want to take unnecessary chances in life, whether for possible gain or, even less so, for the simple thrill of engaging in risky behaviour. This characteristic is not just a result of their senescence; even when they were young, they were more focused on security than today's generation of young people. When the Elders were young, the social safety net whose deterioration we now lament didn't even exist.

The Elders seek stability in all areas of life, and they are more likely than other Canadians to find a sense of comfort in traditional institutions such as churches. They firmly believe in doing unto others as they would have others do unto them. As a result, they are considerably less likely than other Canadians to try to rip off other people or the institutions in which they have faith, whether those institutions are religious, governmental or corporate. They find a sense of stability in being part of a social fabric, an integral part of a community. The Elders tend to pay a lot of attention to what is going on in their local area and to participate in community life, both through institutions and through voluntary associations with others. They want to leave a positive legacy to their children and to society in general, and they're hoping against hope for the restoration of the Judeo-Christian moral codes that provided context and meaning in their early lives. For many of them, Stockwell Day is a promising young whipper-snapper.

Canadian Elders are more likely than members of other generations to believe in hierarchy and patriarchy. They believe there are two more or less permanent classes of people: leaders and followers. In the home, the father is the principal breadwinner, with mother in a supporting role, followed by the children, who are taught to respect authority. The first son is the apple of his father's eye; the first daughter is her mother's help and support. The hierarchy in the home is mirrored in other institutions in their world, whether these are religions (with bishops and priests at their head), industrial or service organizations (led by owners and managers), or professional firms of doctors, lawyers and accountants. For Elders, teachers and police officers are automatically deserving of respect by virtue of their status in society.

Happiness for Canadian Elders is Thanksgiving, a grandchild's wedding, Christmas dinner with the family or other similarly venerated traditions belonging to Canada's myriad faith communities.

For the most part, they have already acquired what they consider to be the necessities of life, and they feel little need to spend for spending's sake or simply to own something new. Indeed, newness in general is not necessarily a plus for them, since they prefer the tried and the tested.

This preference for the traditional goes for relationships as well, and they tend to be opposed to non-traditional living arrangements, such as common-law and especially same-sex relationships. "Adam and Eve, not Adam and Steve" is one way they put it, underlining the fact that their opposition to same-sex relationships is often based on religious considerations. They are also opposed to sexual permissiveness and promiscuity in general, preferring stable relationships to temporary, though sometimes exciting, flings.

The Elders are least likely to say they would like to live in an era in which there is more mystery, romanticism and adventure, perhaps because they understand better than younger people that such eras tend also to be times of danger and instability.

Socio-Cultural Map: Elders 1999

TRADITION

Rational Traditionalists 46%

Extroverted Traditionalists 29%

OTHER-DIRECTED

INNER-DIRECTED

Cosmopolitan Modernists 25%

INDIVIDUALITY

In spite of these generalizations, which can be made based on polling data, there are significant differences among individual Elders. Statistical cluster analysis reveals three distinct social values tribes in this generation: Rational Traditionalists, Extroverted Traditionalists and Cosmopolitan Modernists. The Rational and Extroverted Traditionalists conform more or less to the generational stereotype just presented. The Cosmopolitan Modernists, however, break from that stereotype in many significant ways, and this is testified to by their position way down at the bottom of the socio-cultural map.

Rational Traditionalists
46 Per Cent of Elders; 12 Per Cent of General Population

Key Values	
Strong on	*Weak on*
risk-aversion	adaptability to complexity in life
hyper-rationality	flexibility of gender identity
aversion to complexity in life	pursuit of intensity and emotional experiences
saving on principle	introspection and empathy
everyday ethics	flexible definition of family

As the largest tribe of Elders, the Rational Traditionalists are in many ways typical of their generation, and to some extent determine the profile of Elders in general. Risk-aversion is the value that most differentiates them from other Canadians. Not only are they traditional, but they value rationality highly, largely for the security and stability it can afford. Rational Traditionalists are among the people least likely to let themselves be carried away by their emotions. They go to movies not to have a good cry, but rather to see good triumph over evil.

They are uncomfortable with complexity, and are looking not only for security and stability, but also for clarity and simplicity. Rational Traditionalists save money simply for the sense of security it provides them, even if they have no particular purchase or purpose in mind for their savings. They live by the motto "A penny saved is a penny earned."

Like their generation overall, they tend to value honest and stable relationships with other people and with the institutions with which they do business; they are among the Canadians least likely to try to cheat governments, businesses or their fellow citizens. Though they value money highly for the security it provides, they will not use unethical means to attain it, and they think the world would be a better place if everyone followed their example. The golden rule is for them an article of faith, an embroidered sampler hanging next to their wedding pictures and photos of their grandkids.

This tribe believes deeply in gender roles; both male and female Rational Traditionalists appreciate men acting masculine and women acting feminine—period. The men have, in many cases, sought and found a bride who would stay at home looking after the kids and providing a safe harbour and a warm meal to return to each evening. The women of this tribe are glad they had the chance to raise their children themselves, and they are convinced that mothers who work outside the home for a living cannot help short-changing their families. These women are not frustrated would-be feminists, but rather are generally very satisfied with the security and stability their husbands provided for them.

Rational Traditionalists have a strong sense of what's right and what's wrong, and are sometimes surprised that others don't find things as clear-cut. They rarely make an effort to put themselves in another person's shoes, since "the rules" are universal and should be the same for everyone. They would grant no special status to aggrieved minorities that want the government or the law to right past wrongs. They are particularly unsympathetic towards gay and lesbian partnerships and, to a lesser extent, common-law unions.

Members of this Elder tribe strongly believe that there are times when violence is not only appropriate but necessary. They derided the appeasement strategy of British prime minister Neville Chamberlain, admiring instead Winston

Churchill's resolve to resist the fascist menace. They sub-
scribe to the philosophy of "spare the rod, spoil the child" and
the belief that "the father must be master in his own house."
They are among the nation's strongest supporters of capital
punishment.

Rational Traditionalists' cultural icons are heroes from their
youth: war leaders like the aforementioned Winston Churchill
and Franklin Roosevelt, or the movie star John Wayne, who
was always the good guy and won every war he ever fought,
no matter who the enemy.

Extroverted Traditionalists
29 Per Cent of Elders; 7 Per Cent of General Population

Key Values

Strong on	*Weak on*
search for roots	equal relationship with youth
fear of violence	control of destiny
need for status recognition	importance of spontaneity in daily life
need for personal achievement	pursuit of happiness to the detriment of duty
fatalism	flexible definition of family

Extroverted Traditionalists are best characterized by a strong
search for the comfort of social embeddedness. Located in the
upper-left "Traditional Communities, Institutions and Social
Status" quadrant, they want to feel a sense of belonging and
continuity with the past. They are attached to traditional customs and comportments, and are often very interested in their
genealogy and heritage.

Despite several years of a declining crime rate in Canada,
Extroverted Traditionalists are still quite fearful of violence.
Their alarmism is exacerbated every time they see a headline
in one of the Sun newspapers across the country confirming
their worst fears—including the conviction that young people
are out of control, a fear that is often coupled with a prejudi-

cial wariness of some ethnic minorities. They believe firmly that wisdom comes with age and are opposed vehemently to the liberties accorded teenagers these days. They believe that older people, including themselves, are due a certain degree of respect, because of their individual and collective accomplishments, and simply by virtue of their age.

In the final analysis, social respect is what they crave most of all, and in this they are surprisingly similar to the Tommy Hilfiger–wearing teens they are so quick to criticize. They often do things simply to prove to themselves and to others that they are capable of doing them (although they're careful not to take unnecessary risks).

Extroverted Traditionalists want desperately to feel in control of their lives, but they often feel threatened by what they see as the chaos that lies outside their own households. They are among the Canadians who most strongly believe that beyond their own well-secured property lies a very dangerous and unpredictable world. They dread unforeseen situations, or anything that forces them to change their habits. They like to eat their three meals at the same time every day, with a predictable menu on each day of the week. They dress up for special occasions in the required "uniform"—a pretty dress or a conservative suit—and expect others to do the same. They are among the most conscientious Canadians, devoted to the ideas of Christian charity, duty and noblesse oblige, and they almost always do what they think is morally right, even if it inconveniences them. Some may find their values to be quaint in our cynical era, but few would criticize them as being hypocritical.

Family is at the centre of Extroverted Traditionalists' lives, and the women of this tribe are its custodians. They maintain regular telephone contact with their children; birthdays of grandchildren are conscientiously acknowledged with cards and gifts, and plans for family gatherings are made months in advance. For these people, religious services are also important, not just for the spiritual solace they offer, but also for the social activities and charitable initiatives that accompany them.

The icons of the Extroverted Traditionalists are religious figures like Mother Teresa or the Pope, Hyacinth Bucket (pronounced Bouquet) from *Keeping Up Appearances*, a Britcom North Americans love, classic mother and father figures from the family sitcoms of the 1950s and 1960s, and our prime minister.

Cosmopolitan Modernists
25 Per Cent of Elders; 6 Per Cent of General Population

Key Values	
Strong on	*Weak on*
new social responsibility	connectivity
control of destiny	fear of violence
rejection of authority	acceptance of violence
community involvement	importance of
everyday ethics	national superiority
	need for status recognition

Cosmopolitan Modernists most clearly distinguish themselves from Canadians at large in their strong concern for those less fortunate. They are the winners of their generation, and they feel a personal responsibility to help those who have been less successful, a group that may include their own children. When the Cosmopolitan Modernists were young, they were smart and diligent. They did well in school, and when they got out, in many cases with a post-secondary education, they worked hard and have on the whole achieved considerable success, whether as the family's principal breadwinner or as the chatelaine of an upper-middle-class household. They have been prudent with their money and can look forward to a very comfortable retirement.

CosMods feel a strong sense of personal control over their own lives and tend to question rather than blindly accept the edicts of authority figures. Because they're often in positions of power themselves, they realize that even those with the best intentions sometimes make mistakes. They are proponents of progress and reform, and believe these are accomplished only through the judicious questioning of the status quo. Cosmopolitan Modernists were often the first people in their families to quietly question religious authority. Even if they continued to seek spiritual growth in conventional religious practices, many were also understanding, even sympathetic, when their rebellious Baby Boomer children decided to leave the faith.

Cosmopolitan Modernists pay close attention to what is happening both around the world and in their own community, and they tend to think and act both locally and globally. They are the leading Canadian citizens of the global village. Like their generation in general, they harbour a strong sense of personal ethics, and are among the least likely to try to rip off the business and government institutions that have often contributed to their personal success. They have always believed in playing by the rules, whether those rules belong to the game of golf or the game of life. They have benefited extensively from the current system, not by cheating the other guy, but by hard work and the application of ethical values. The system, they believe, is basically good, and they are motivated to make it even better. They believe that reform of the system should be ongoing, but they are certainly not interested in overthrowing it. Their idealism is pragmatic, not revolutionary.

Though Cosmopolitan Modernists are sociable, they are not particularly gregarious and are less likely than others to appreciate mass gatherings like sports events or informal concerts. They enjoy their season's tickets to the theatre, opera or ballet and their membership in the art gallery or museum, but they prefer to socialize in more intimate venues with smaller groups of their own choosing. They are neither intimidated by nor accepting of violence, and see physical aggression as a completely unacceptable way to resolve disputes. In temperament, they are much more UN than NATO, more Maurice Strong than Norman Schwarzkopf. Perhaps not surprisingly, they are among the least flag-waving of Canadians. Though proud of our country, they are aware that cultures and

countries have different strong and weak points, and they
have no illusions that Canada has a monopoly on morality or
on quality of life. They have travelled more than other
Canadians, have friends in other countries, keep up with the
news and are able to put things in context.

Cosmopolitan Modernists are also among the Canadians
least interested in going out of their way to win the respect of
others. Once you've achieved a certain level of respect, as is
the case with security and stability, you cease to strive for it as
feverishly. The Cosmopolitan Modernists feel that they
already have the respect of those who are important to them,
and they are not interested in further status-seeking. They do
not need to see their names chiselled in marble on monu-
ments to know they've made it.

The men in this tribe are proud of their accomplished
daughter with her Harvard MBA, but they also have profound
love and respect for the wife who stayed home to raise their
children. Both spouses are proud of all their children, whatever they have chosen to do with their lives.

The singular Canadian icon of this generation is the
guy who slid down the banister into our ballot boxes in 1968,
the Right Honourable Pierre Elliott Trudeau. To paraphrase
his biographers Christina McCall and Stephen Clarkson, he
haunts them still.

The Boomers—40 Per Cent of Canadian Population

Key Values	
Strong on	*Weak on*
racing against the clock	attraction for crowds
flexible definition of family	reprioritizing of money
control of destiny	penchant for risk-taking
financial concern for the future	pursuit of originality
strategic consumption	ostentatious consumption

As a generation, the Boomers are most characterized by how
busy they are—with work, with family, with personal fulfill-

ment. They are more likely than members of other generations to say there is never enough time in a day to get everything done. This, of course, makes sense for the generation that en masse said to itself: "We are not going to live like our parents. They lived lives of duty and self-sacrifice for their parents, for their spouses and for us, their children, deferring gratification till their old age or till the next life. We're determined to have more than a little fun on the way through." Well, if as a generation you're going to make time for serious fun, in addition to stepping up your work schedule, having kids and all but universalizing the dual-income household, you'd better be wearing comfortable shoes. Many Boomers have found that in trying to cram so much into one lifetime, they have bitten off much more than they can chew.

In general, Boomers are liberal in their ideas about family structure, generally accepting the legitimacy of common-law and same-sex relationships. When the federal government introduced legislation granting same-sex relationships a status equivalent to that of opposite-sex common-law relationships, most Boomers didn't bat an eye. Despite the fact that they are harried and stressed, they feel that their lives are, and always have been, in their control, and they think others should be accorded the right to that same control. Their individualism is accompanied by a certain degree of empathy for others and by the ideals of equality and social justice. Their idealism is reminiscent of the New Testament admonition that only he who is without sin should cast the first stone.

Having finally faced the fact that they are now in middle age, Boomers are increasingly thinking about how they will fare during their retirement. They are focusing more on substance and less on style, and are willing to switch to less expensive brands or shop more carefully, time permitting. The older Boomers, those who are now in their late forties and early fifties, are wondering if they really need more "things" at this stage in their lives, and they are even considering downsizing (both homes and lifestyles), particularly if the kids have more or less left home, placing them on the threshold of becoming empty-nesters. Mainstream Boomers are not trying to stand out from or fit into the crowd through their consumption of material goods—they are simply doing their own thing as they always have. Having other people admire their possessions is the least of their worries since many people in their generation created their own symbols of status and self-worth, rather than simply accepting the conventional dictates of society.

Despite this relative indifference to the material trappings of success, Boomers are very focused on making money, and are even willing to sacrifice some of their treasured personal autonomy if it means more dollars. They are beyond the age of taking chances with their future and are averse to taking high-stakes risks, limiting themselves to the minor vice of the lottery. Mutual funds are the financial vehicle of choice for those with the means, although many are frustrated by their recent lacklustre performance at a time when some dot-com equity stocks have been going through the roof.

Socio-Cultural Map: Boomers 1999

TRADITION

Anxious Communitarians 15%

Disengaged Darwinists 43%

OTHER-DIRECTED

INNER-DIRECTED

Connected Enthusiasts 15%

Autonomous Rebels 27%

INDIVIDUALITY

Consistent with their stereotype, Boomers tend to be individualistic and not overly gregarious. They are no longer interested in large events, except maybe on DVD, and are busy enough and happy enough in smaller groups involving their families, loved ones and the few friends they still have time to see. However, as with the Elders, not all Boomers fit the same mould. In fact, statistical cluster analysis reveals four distinct social values tribes of Baby Boomers: Autonomous Rebels, Connected Enthusiasts, Disengaged Darwinists and Anxious Communitarians.

Autonomous Rebels
27 Per Cent of Boomers; 11 Per Cent of General Population

Key Values

Strong on	Weak on
rejection of authority	ostentatious consumption
control of destiny	concern for appearance
equal relationship with youth	importance of national superiority
importance of spontaneity in daily life	search for roots
adaptability to complexity in life	need for status recognition

Autonomous Rebels are the quintessential Boomers, what we at Environics call the defining segment of their generation. They are best characterized by their inclination to question, rather than blindly accept, authority. As well, they are more at ease with complexity, diversity and change than any of their elders or age peers, and if asking questions makes things more complicated, so be it. This tribe has never been able to hold its tongue.

Autonomous Rebels insist on maintaining a sense of control over their personal destiny. This manifests itself in everything from choosing their own path in life to taking a break at work and going for a coffee or a cigarette when they choose. Personal choice is the cornerstone of their mental posture.

Autonomous Rebels tend to be more egalitarian than other Canadians. In their youth, the early Boomers empathized with the U.S. civil-rights movement, and they eagerly encouraged the application of the principles of social justice to women and ethnic minorities in this country in the 1960s and 1970s. Now in middle age, they are more likely than other Canadians to extend their egalitarian idealism to teenagers, according them the same rights and responsibilities as everyone else. Often having been raised in fairly traditional homes and communities, the Rebels remember what it is like to be a young person denied the freedom and respect given to other members of society. So profound was their own youthful idealism that they are still able to sympathize with young people, even with their own teenage children. In their youth, they didn't trust anyone over thirty. Over time, that stance has broadened to become a generalized scepticism about most individuals and almost all institutions. In the end, Autonomous Rebels have often concluded that you can really trust only yourself in this life.

Though for the most part successful, the Autonomous Rebels are not interested in showing off; they tend to find prominent labels ("walking billboards") to be in extremely bad taste, a pathetic submission to the manipulation of cynical consumer marketers preying on the ingenuous and the insecure. They don't like their country to show off either. Like the Cosmopolitan Modernists, Autonomous Rebels are proud Canadians, but they have no illusions about our country being an international Boy Scout. They don't wave the Canadian flag, and they don't wave the figurative flag of whatever ethnic group they happen to belong to. Canada may be the best country in the world, but it will stay that way only if we uphold our heritage of understatement and don't brag about it. They are nationalistic but not patriotic. Patriots are willing to die for their country; these Rebels don't want to die for anything—they want to live for everything. For Autonomous Rebels, an individual is just that—an individual—and is not to be stereotyped on the basis of race or nationality. Also like the Cosmopolitan Modernists, Autonomous Rebels already have the respect of the people whose opinions they care about, and they don't exert themselves to win over others.

Their cultural icons include the Beatles, particularly John Lennon, who composed "Imagine," the unofficial anthem of their tribe, the feminist Gloria Steinem, the scientist/environmentalist David Suzuki and the political visionary Nelson Mandela. All these people are idealists who represent a vision of a better world. The male members of this tribe identified with the Kevin Spacey character in the 1999 hit movie *American Beauty*, often enjoying a last blast of self-indulgent laxity as part of their mid-life crisis before permanently adopting the more evolved brand of thoughtful individualism towards which they have been moving since their youth.

Anxious Communitarians
15 Per Cent of Boomers; 6 Per Cent of General Population

Key Values	
Strong on	*Weak on*
ostentatious consumption	rejection of order
need for status recognition	new social responsibility
joy of consumption	control of destiny
concern for appearance	rejection of authority
importance of national superiority	hyper-rationality

Anxious Communitarians are, of all Canadians, those most interested in keeping up with, or better yet outdoing, the Joneses. In terms of values, they are diametrically opposed to the Autonomous Rebels. For Anxious Communitarians, status is crucial, and they crave the admiration of others not only for themselves but for their possessions. They love shopping; buying themselves something new is one of their greatest pleasures in life. They are card-carrying members of the "dress for success" school so brilliantly captured by Annette Bening in the aforementioned *American Beauty*, and clothes are as much a priority for them as they are for image-obsessed teens. The labels may be different, but the motivations are the same. They are very proud of their nationality and are big flag-wavers, viewing the maple leaf (or the fleur-de-lys in Quebec) as yet another prestigious label belonging to them.

It is important for Anxious Communitarians to have everything neat, tidy and in its proper place. It is essential for the home to be tastefully appointed, and for guests to be impressed by its modern amenities and tiny details of decor. Neighbours and passersby who are not invited inside at least receive an implicit invitation to admire the smart styling of the new car in the driveway or the sparkling pool in the backyard. This tribe celebrates the day that Martha Stewart, the cultural maven of modern bourgeois good taste, first made her presence felt in their lives.

Members of this group are considerably more complacent and even smug than they were a few years ago. Anxious Communitarians are people who have largely given up on the idea of social justice, and they are resigned to the fact that there will always be poverty. They feel that events are largely determined by fate, and that people have little control over the way things go. Consequently, they do not feel at all guilty about their relative good fortune, and are in fact relieved that it is others who have to do without. *Jerry Springer* is among their favourite TV programs because it reminds them that their own troubles pale in comparison with those of the miserable wretches they see on the show.

Anxious Communitarians tend to be very emotional and rarely spend time analyzing or thinking critically about issues. They are not at all into rocking the boat, and tend to defer to authority without questioning it. They have supreme confidence in the police and in politicians who reflect their interests, such as Ontario premier Mike Harris.

With the exception of Martha Stewart, their cultural icons are drawn from the world of televised talk shows, sitcoms and romantic movies. These include Oprah Winfrey, Julia Roberts, and the pop singers Paul Anka, Neil Diamond and Barry

Manilow, whose middle-of-the-road sentimentalism is literally music to Anxious Communitarians' ears.

Connected Enthusiasts
15 Per Cent of Boomers; 6 Per Cent of General Population

Key Values	
Strong on	*Weak on*
introspection and empathy	acceptance of violence
discriminating consumerism	hyper-rationality
intuitive potential	ostentatious consumption
sensualism	aimlessness
personal creativity	anomie

If the Anxious Communitarians have become a little cold-hearted on their way to the mall, the Connected Enthusiasts have become more sympathetic to others in their voyage of self-discovery. These are people who really empathize with others, and are able to put themselves in another person's shoes. Not surprisingly, they totally reject violence as a means of settling disputes, and are even turned off by violent movies and television. It is not that they are conservative—they're not—but they are sensitive to the role the environment plays in their own and others' physical and psychological well-being. They believe everyone should be given the opportunity to fulfill his or her potential, and they put their money and their actions where their mouths are. They consider themselves creative people, and often try to express this creativity in their work or hobbies. They have a strong sense of both direction and social connectedness in life.

Like Anxious Communitarians, Connected Enthusiasts tend to be very emotional, but they are not at all status-seeking. In fact, they often reject the consumerism they see around them, judging it to be unrestrained and vulgar. They are careful shoppers, and shop for what they need, at the best price, rather than for what their neighbours will find most impressive. They are experiential rather than material hedonists, and are often influenced as much by the way something feels as by the way it looks. Hearing, taste and smell are also vital senses for this tribe. These are the poly-sensuous Boomers. They wish to explore different aspects of their personalities, to play with different facets of their identi-ties. In their youth, they celebrated the sexual revolution and the birth control pill, approving of the chemical tool that allowed them to do with their bodies what they wished, when they wished, without fear of pregnancy. As they have aged and their libidos and opportunities have diminished, their soft hedonism has expressed itself in an exploration of sensuality and a quest for personal discovery. Their goals in life include achieving emotional intensity and pursuing the authentic.

Connected Enthusiasts' cultural icons are the many lives of Shirley MacLaine, Celine Dion and the cast of Denys Arcand's *Decline of the American Empire*.

Disengaged Darwinists
43 Per Cent of Boomers; 17 Per Cent of General Population

Key Values	
Strong on	*Weak on*
financial concern regarding the future	adaptability to complexity in life
hyper-rationality	pursuit of intensity and emotional experiences
saving on principle	
aversion to complexity in life	connectivity
confidence in advertising	need for personal achievement
	sensualism

In the mid-1990s, the Disengaged Darwinists were best de-scribed, if a bit sweepingly, as "angry white guys." Now, in the new millennium, a better description is perhaps "fright-ened white guys." Of course, there are plenty of women in this tribe too, though men are still overrepresented. These are people who, a few years ago, first became unhappy with the way the world was heading—growing complexity, increasing multiculturalism, globalization, new technology and a huge premium on being well educated—and they felt that their (often blue-collar) contribution was being ignored or under-valued. They saw their own jobs being threatened by forces beyond their control as Canada adopted free trade with the U.S. and then quickly fell into the deepest recession it has known since the Great Depression of the 1930s. They wit-nessed the continuing immigration of people of various ethnicities into Canada, and they viewed the social safety net as a service paid for by their taxes but designed for someone else's benefit. Government policies of bilingualism, pay equity and affirmative action only added insult to injury. They were angry, and they weren't going to take it any more. The under-dog became the underwolf and wanted to bite back, if only with its reactionary vote.

Five years later, it has become apparent that these forces are here to stay, regardless of Disengaged Darwinists' reac-tion to them, and this tribe's anger is now accompanied by fear. They are most worried about bottom-line questions like their own financial future and how they're going to put bread on the table, particularly those who have lost their jobs or feel that their jobs are vulnerable. Money gives them a sense of security, and they often save it "for a rainy day," with no par-ticular purchase in mind.

Despite their anger and fear, Disengaged Darwinists try desperately to keep their emotions in check, and to look at things as rationally as possible. The sensuous holds little attraction for them. More than anything else, they want secu-rity, stability and clarity in all areas of life. They are not interested in sharing group emotions or finding "the child within," and they basically keep to themselves and their fam-ilies. They don't have anything to prove to anyone. They just want to keep their heads above water until the day the gov-ernment lowers their taxes, deports illegal immigrants and reinstitutes capital punishment.

Their cultural icons are the hockey great Gordie Howe, who was good and tough; the sports commentator Don

Cherry; actors like Chuck Norris, Jean-Claude Van Damme and their many male Hollywood surrogates; and the *Married with Children* character Al Bundy. In the political arena, they cheer whenever a right-wing demagogue tells it like it is.

Generation X—35 Per Cent of Canadian Population

Key Values	
Strong on	*Weak on*
penchant for risk-taking	risk-aversion
acceptance of violence	discriminating consumerism
enthusiasm for consumption	everyday ethics
sexual permissiveness	religiosity
equal relationship with youth	attraction to the simple pleasures of life

The post-Boomers, those born after 1964 and popularly known as Generation X, are the most diverse of the generations in terms of socio-cultural values. The youngest Gen Xers in our current 1999 sample were born in the mid-1980s. This generation of young Canadians has grown up in a period of rapid social, economic and technological change in the three decades at the end of the twentieth century. The values tribes that this generation comprises range all the way from the most idealistic of all Canadians, the New Aquarians, to the most nihilistic people in the country, the Aimless Dependants. Readers of *Sex in the Snow* will be interested to learn that the analysis for this book uncovered not only the five original youth tribes, but also reveals a new tribe that emerged in the late 1990s: the Security-seeking Ascetics.

Taken as a group and compared with previous generations, this is the "sex, drugs and rock 'n' roll" generation, or increasingly, the "sex, tech and rap" generation. The values Gen Xers are strongest on are associated with excitement and risk-taking. More than their elders, they are willing to take chances, both to get what they want out of life and simply for the fun of it. They are often excited by violent television programs or violent films such as *Seven*, *Fight Club* and *Gladiator*, or the thoroughly ironic *Scream* movies, which exploit the palpable eroticism of a beautiful but terrified young woman. They are enthusiastic consumers who keep on the lookout for new things and experiences. Their attention spans are shorter than those of previous generations, and their lives seem focused on the pursuit of emotionally intense jolts, which are easy to find in the world of virtual reality.

Not surprisingly, Gen Xers are the group of Canadians most likely to say that young people should be accorded the same rights, privileges and freedoms as their elders. They feel less attached to institutions, and sometimes even to their fellow Canadians, than do their elders, and as a result are willing to rip off governments and corporations if given the opportunity. Deterrents to this sort of behaviour are not so much moral as logistical: it's a question not of whether to cheat but of how to avoid getting caught. Though many Gen Xers believe in God, their attachment to religious institutions tends to be weak or non-existent, and their conception of God is amorphous and often self-serving. The devil is viewed not as a threat, but as either a joke or the icon of the bad (that is, the fun).

Though often strapped for cash, Gen Xers tend not to shop around or comparison shop; they are motivated by a desire for immediate, as opposed to deferred, gratification. In spite of the stereotype of all Gen Xers as lacking a cause or a sense of direction or meaning, they are coming to be recognized as a fascinating cohort. In their lifetimes, they have enjoyed or suffered the legacy of their Baby Boomer parents, a roller-coaster economy and an explosion of technological innovations, not the least of which are the hundred-channel cable universe, the personal computer and the Internet. Statistical cluster analysis reveals them to be even more diverse than the Baby Boomers, and for that reason alone they are more interesting. They are also much more difficult for the marketers of consumer products and services to target accurately.

Although there are only three tribes of Elders and four tribes of Baby Boomers, we find in our current analysis no fewer than

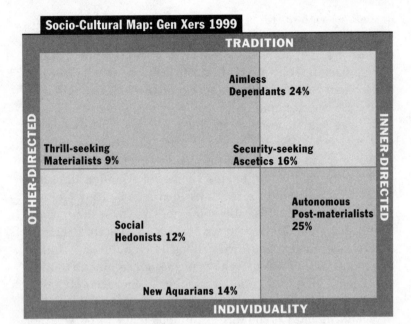

six tribes of Gen Xers: Autonomous Post-materialists, New Aquarians, Social Hedonists, Thrill-seeking Materialists, Aimless Dependants and Security-seeking Ascetics. This last tribe, which is only now emerging into the spotlight to assert its distinction from the other tribes of young people, is certainly one of the most fascinating.

Aimless Dependants
24 Per Cent of Gen X; 8 Per Cent of General Population

Key Values	
Strong on	*Weak on*
ostentatious consumption	adaptability to complexity in life
acceptance of violence	
importance of national superiority	rejection of authority
	new social responsibility
attraction for crowds	equality of the sexes
civil disobedience	fulfillment through work

Over the past several years, Aimless Dependants have become considerably more ostentatious in their consumption. While they were always focused on fitting in, members of this tribe now think the easiest way to conform is to wear the right brands and have the right material possessions. Some brands that are popular among teenagers, such as Nike, Hilfiger or Gap, are familiar standbys, but hip-hop brands such as FUBU, Ecko, Phat Farm and others are also gaining popularity.

Even among a generation that is excited by violent entertainment, the Aimless Dependants are exceptional. Members of this tribe enjoy violent movies and television programs, as well as violent sports and video games, such as Mortal Kombat. In the worst circumstances, Aimless Dependants are excited by violence—period. This tribe was ecstatic to hear that the World Wrestling Federation may sponsor a new football league, and felt that Marty McSorley's suspension for attempted decapitation of a fellow hockey player with his stick was excessive punishment. After all, hockey isn't for wimps; if you can't take the hits, get off the ice.

This is a tribe characterized by aimlessness and anomie. Members' lives lack meaning, and they feel little or no connection with the institutions they have encountered so far, such as family, school and the world of work. Their attachment to other people is often pretty superficial. Because they don't feel very good about themselves, they find it hard to feel good about anyone else.

Aimless Dependants enjoy large group experiences such as concerts and major sporting events, but their love of the crowd is narcissistic, not empathetic. They may enjoy the powerful rush of being in the midst of a seething mass of humanity, but they care little about the individuals who make up a concert audience, a ballpark crowd or any other group, for that matter. They say they have enough trouble looking after themselves without worrying about less fortunate members of society. They are also more likely than other

Canadians to harbour sexist stereotypes and attitudes, and these are often accompanied by an exaggerated virile bluster.

This tribe is full of flag-wavers who are eager to prove to the world that Canada is number one (or in *la belle province*, that Quebec is number one), or more broadly, that their particular ethnic ancestry is number one. Despite this apparent patriotism, Aimless Dependants are more likely than other Canadians to say that it's okay to cheat on your taxes, and that it's okay to disobey a law if you think it is stupid. Many of these Gen Xers smoked and drank when they were underage, and they don't hesitate to smoke (or even grow) marijuana if they feel like it.

Aimless Dependants are ill at ease with diversity, and not surprisingly feel more and more detached from our increasingly complex society and the world in general. More than their age peers, they are nostalgic for the "good old days," a time when things were simple, when those with little education could get well-paid jobs by virtue of their brawn; a time when "men were men and women were women," when men played sports and women were in the swimsuit edition; a time when there were just wars to be fought by brave men. Yes, these perspectives still survive in some young people, and there is plenty of content in our popular culture that appeals to their prejudices, paranoia and stereotypes. That said, the "good old days" (and whether such days ever actually existed is questionable) and the associated values no longer enjoy universal social approval, and the force of these ideals is dwindling over time. They are a dying breed and they sense it.

Perhaps not surprisingly for a tribe whose members have a limited skill set, job security and salary are the main motivation in the world of work. For these Gen Xers, personal fulfillment is a distant secondary consideration—just give them a job and show them the money.

Their cultural icons include the most nihilistic bands of the hour: at the time of this writing, including Korn, Limp Bizkit and Slipknot, as well as various figures in the genre of gangsta rap.

Thrill-seeking Materialists
9 Per Cent of Gen X; 3 Per Cent of General Population

Key Values	
Strong on	*Weak on*
connectivity	hyper-rationality
sensualism	control of destiny
pursuit of novelty	rejection of authority
search for roots	aversion to complexity in life
need for personal achievement	scepticism towards small business

Since *Sex in the Snow* was published a few years ago, the Thrill-seeking Materialists have remained singular in their quest for thrills, but their in-your-face materialism is now being shared by the Aimless Dependants.

Thrill-seeking Materialists love group emotions at large events such as concerts and raves. They tend to be very sensuous, and it is important to them that all of their senses be stimulated by an experience. In terms of products, they want whatever is fresh, the newest, the latest, and they are loath to be seen with anything outmoded, from their clothes to their cellphone. Like their fellow denizens of the upper-left-hand quadrant of our socio-cultural map, the Anxious Communitarians of the Baby Boom generation and the Extroverted Traditionalists of the Elders, Thrill-seeking Materialists are at home in the mall, shopping for new things that will impress their friends.

As some of the most other-directed of all Canadians, Thrill-seeking Materialists place great importance on the opinions of other people, and they often do things just to prove to others (and sometimes to themselves) that they are capable. They tend to be more attached to their ethnic heritage and roots than are most people their age. In fact, recent immigrants are slightly overrepresented among Thrill-seeking Materialists as they strive to gain the acceptance of their peers by departing from the traditional values of their parents and embracing the conspicuous consumption that is the hall-mark of modernity.

These Gen Xers tend to look at things from a more emotional, less rational perspective. They feel that they, and people in general, have little control over their own destinies, so there is little reason to rock the boat or agitate for change. Overall, they express above-average confidence in most institutions, especially businesses that deliver the goods they covet, and they question authority only rarely.

Their cultural icons are the mainstream heroes in the worlds of popular music, televised sitcoms, movies and professional sports, especially the ever-popular Michael Jordan, and top hip-hop and rap performers.

New Aquarians
14 Per Cent of Gen X; 5 Per Cent of General Population

Key Values	
Strong on	*Weak on*
adaptability to complexity in life	risk-aversion
flexibility of gender identity	aversion to complexity in life
pursuit of originality	hyper-rationality
interest in the mysterious	ostentatious consumption
connectivity	saving on principle

New Aquarians, who can be found in the lower-left "Experience-seeking and New Frontiers" quadrant of the socio-cultural map, are among the most adaptable and least fearful of Canadians, financially and otherwise. They are the intellectual, if not the actual, children of the Autonomous Rebel tribe in the Baby Boom generation, but they are even more idealistic than the eponymous Rebels were in their day. Examples of New Aquarians in action include the APEC demonstrators who were pepper-sprayed in Vancouver a few years ago, as well as the young Canadians who made their way to Seattle, Washington, D.C., and Windsor in late 1999 and early 2000 to oppose the policies of the World Trade Organization, the International Monetary Fund, the World Bank and the Organization of American States. In addition to embracing traditional methods of protest, New Aquarians are blazing trails with new modes of civil disobedience, including computer "hacktivism" (computer hacking with an ethical purpose). The New Aquarians carry on the counter-cultural tradition of the hippies, and the beats before them, as the true outsiders in our midst.

New Aquarians like to experiment with different aspects of their personalities, and they reject the limitations of traditional gender roles—making this tribe the diametrical opposites of the Aimless Dependants. Among their friends, they number, or aspire to number, every race, colour and creed, as well as gays, bisexuals and others who are different from the mainstream. They are extremely gregarious and enjoy spending time with family, friends and strangers, in person or on-line. Environics has labelled them "New Aquarians" because they harbour many of the values associated with the much-heralded Age of Aquarius and are in many ways leading the way to a uto-pian future. They are interested in forces that can't yet be explained by science, and are also often interested in expres-sions of spirituality and mysticism that are not mainstream in the West—Buddhism, yoga, astrology and Native American spirituality.

Of all Canadians, New Aquarians are the quintessential early adopters, but this does not mean that they will always be the first to buy new brands. They are early adopters of new ways of doing things, which sometimes involves new products and sometimes involves the rejection of new products. They are the cool young people who are now getting their clothes at second-hand, army surplus and Goodwill stores—not because of financial constraints, but because they reject what they see as vulgar and unethical consumerism, as represented by Nike, the Gap, Tommy Hilfiger and other brands popular with their age peers. Their world-view is much more Greenpeace than greenbacks.

The *No Logo* author Naomi Klein has identified an arche-typal New Aquarian phenomenon: the student anti-sweatshop movement that has sprung up on more than two hundred campuses across North America. Despite the stereo-type of Generation X as a passive throng of branded-logo tribes, these student activists are demanding accountability, transparency and social responsibility from multinational brands like Nike and Coke. They insist that the colleges and universities that do lucrative deals with multinationals push these suppliers to pay decent living wages to the workers who produce their products in Third World sweatshops. Who said idealism was dead?

Their cultural icons range from Gandhi to Chomsky to Naomi Klein. For the philosophically minded, postmodern philosophers Michel Foucault and Gilles Deleuze are favourites. In the world of pop culture, New Aquarians favour celebrities like Sarah McLachlan of Lilith Fair fame and the Beastie Boys, who espouse the Free Tibet crusade.

Autonomous Post-materialists
25 Per Cent of Gen X; 9 Per Cent of General Population

Key Values	
Strong on	*Weak on*
equal relationship with youth	search for roots
acceptance of violence	discriminating consumerism
importance of spontaneity in daily life	primacy of the family
scepticism towards small business	fear of violence
rejection of order	financial concern for the future

For Autonomous Post-materialists, it all boils down to one fun-damental value: freedom. This means individual freedom, including freedom from control by government, business and even one's parents. Like the New Aquarians, they are the intellectual descendants of the Autonomous Rebels of the

Boomer generation, but they often lack the idealism of their New Aquarian peers. When they were young, the Autonomous Rebels wished to assert themselves and advance the cause of social justice. Autonomous Post-materialists certainly wish to assert themselves, but not politically. Instead, they are much more likely to assert themselves in the classroom and in the world of business. Few aspire to public service. They take for granted the egalitarian advances for which the Autonomous Rebels fought, and instead they are now fighting for themselves in an increasingly global, competitive and Darwinist world. They have no time for anachronistic political games, appeals to the "common good" or revolutionary change.

Quintessential examples of this tribe are two Toronto teenagers, Michael Furdyk and Jennifer Corriero, who claim to have been hard-wired to the Internet since birth and already have a number of Internet initiatives under their belts. They went to Seattle to conduct a six-month consumer research project on the work needs and methods of people in their late teens and early twenties—the Net Gen—on behalf of Microsoft's Next Generation Knowledge Worker project. And they are not doing it for minimum wage. At the age of sixteen, Furdyk had already sold an Internet publishing company for well into seven figures.

Autonomous Post-materialists believe that young people are perfectly capable of making their own decisions in life, and they have no patience for any form of paternalism or hierarchy. They are very aggressive and tend to be excited by, and not at all fearful of, violent media (although violence itself is rare in their everyday experience). They want the freedom to do what they want, when and where they want. They are not sticklers for propriety, and prefer casual and messy comfort to structured neatness. A loft in Toronto or in New York's SoHo is their ideal of a cool living space.

Autonomous Post-materialists are less confident than other Canadians in the goodwill and honesty of business. Why, they ask, should they be loyal to a company—or for that matter, a country—when such an institution would never be loyal to them? Isn't that the world Canadians opted for when we bought free trade from Brian Mulroney in 1988? Members of this tribe are not consumerist, nor are they particularly scrupulous when making purchases. In fact, they are disinterested in the whole consumer experience, and are more into spontaneity than careful research when it comes to their day-to-day purchases. Like members of the other most modern youth tribe, the New Aquarians, Autonomous Post-materialists tend not to be fearful in general, especially where money is concerned.

Autonomous Post-materialists are among the least nostalgic and sentimental of Canadians, and they think that one's ethnic heritage, including their own, is largely irrelevant. For them, we are all human beings first, and whatever comes second is either incidental or freely chosen. They are strong proponents of fundamental human rights, as pursued by groups like Amnesty International and the Canadian Civil Liberties Association, although unlike their New Aquarian cousins, they are generally too busy to actually get involved in these groups. They have little use for the "political correctness" most of the New Aquarians embrace.

Though in general all the tribes value the family, Autonomous Post-materialists are less sentimental than others, and are more likely to say that there are sometimes other things in their lives that are more important, such as their personal freedom, their principles and their work. These are not the rugged individualists who bought into the often violent, dog-eat-dog world of social Darwinism, but they are individualists all the same.

Their cultural icons are New Economy capitalists like Apple Computer's Steve Jobs and the "masters of the universe" on New York's Wall Street. Other icons include singer/songwriter/entrepreneur/feminist Ani Difranco, Canadian pop music group Sloan and anyone else who has succeeded by doing his own thing and not being hindered by the opinions of others.

Social Hedonists
12 Per Cent of Gen X; 4 Per Cent of General Population

Key Values	
Strong on	*Weak on*
adaptability to complexity in life	primacy of the family
pursuit of novelty	hyper-rationality
penchant for risk-taking	risk-aversion
pursuit of intensity and emotional experiences	saving on principle
connectivity	control of destiny

In their motivations, Social Hedonists are the most experiential of all Canadians. Their mental posture, combined with the natural vitality of their youth, makes them Canadian society's ultimate party animals. They live for today—and tonight too. They are at ease with, and even relish, complexity, and are constantly in search of novelty. They are willing to take chances on the untried, untested and untrue, and are ruled by their hearts more than their heads. They love large group events and all-night parties. Their Saturday night fever often extends to two, three or even four other nights of the week.

When not surrounded by, chatting with or e-mailing their numerous friends, Social Hedonists are terminally bored; they find nothing less appetizing than the thought of having to return to their families and their work after a party. Sleep is an inconvenient necessity of life that they often minimize as much as possible. They live by that familiar paean to immediate gratification "Eat, drink and be merry, for tomorrow we die." But in the case of Social Hedonists, other drugs sometimes replace the drink, and the eating part takes place only when it doesn't interfere with the rest of their social agenda. They feel they have little control over their lives, and they are here for a good time, not necessarily a long time. Not surprisingly, they are not interested in saving for the future, and instead are much more engaged by seeing if they can successfully apply for yet another credit card. They rarely think about or plan for their old age.

Their cultural icons are, for females, whoever is on the cover of *Cosmo*, *Vogue* or, for the younger set, *Seventeen*, *YM*, *Teen* and *Teen People* magazines. The boys are amused by the playful self-indulgence of magazines like *Wallpaper** and *Maxim*. Both sexes in this tribe admire top DJs, and they enjoy nothing so much as a good rave.

Security-seeking Ascetics
16 Per Cent of Gen X; 6 Per Cent of General Population

Key Values	
Strong on	*Weak on*
saving on principle	adaptability to complexity in life
financial concern for the future	
openness towards others	importance of national superiority
primacy of the family	
equality of the sexes	flexibility of personality
	ostentatious consumption
	pursuit of intensity and emotional experiences

Environics had not yet identified the Security-seeking Ascetics when *Sex in the Snow* was published at the beginning of 1997—that is, they had not emerged in significant enough numbers in the mid-1990s to be categorized as a distinct youth tribe. But over the past five years, they did become distinct. In terms of values, these security-seekers are in many ways diametrically opposed to the Social Hedonists. For the Social Hedonists life is all about immediate gratification, but for the Security-seeking Ascetics it is about deferred gratification. This is the tribe where you find people starting RRSPs in their late twenties, if not earlier.

This tribe includes some of the Aimless Dependants, Thrill-seeking Materialists and Social Hedonists found in our 1995 analysis. These Gen Xers have adapted to an increas-

ingly Darwinist world by doing the civilian equivalent of joining the army: they've decided to hunker down and sign up for
conformity. As a result, they have now, for the first time in
many years, found some meaning in their lives. Junior has
finally emerged from the basement; he's got religion, a job, a
barber and his own apartment. And now he's looking for a
wife. Hallelujah!

Security-seeking Ascetics are similar to the Aimless
Dependants in that members of both tribes are searching for
financial independence, security and stability. But while the
Aimless Dependants don't know how to achieve this security,
and currently have little chance of doing so, the Security-
seeking Ascetics are actually acting on this desire, denying
themselves now so that they won't have to worry later in life.
These people have taken quite seriously the lyrics to
Fleetwood Mac's "Don't Stop Thinking about Tomorrow."

They are fundamentally conservative in their lifestyle.
Their family is the top priority in life, and they are so focused
on achieving financial success because they want to be able
to provide their current or planned spouse and children with a
comfortable and worry-free life. Unlike most people in previous generations who conform to these traditional values, they
are strong believers in the equality of the sexes, both at home
and at work, and consider their relationship a loving and
equal partnership that provides a lot of the security they
crave. They are not interested in exploring their emotions and
different aspects of their personalities, preferring instead a
down-to-earth and rational stability.

They crave security partly because they have a harder
time dealing with complexity than other people their age.
Like the Aimless Dependants, they would really like clarity
and simplicity. They distinguish themselves from the Aimless
Dependants with their lack of interest in either labels or flag-
waving, which they find a bit too hyperbolic and over the top
for their modest tastes and ambitious long-term plans.

However, espousing conventional wisdom at an uncon-
ventional time in history may be financial suicide. The

Security-seeking Ascetics are not the ones making fortunes on NASDAQ—they are too averse to complexity and not sufficiently adaptable. In fact the Autonomous Rebels and the Cosmopolitan Modernists are the ones doing well in today's market. Despite being the most financially obsessed, the Security-seeking Ascetics are old school; they are the ones who are into "sure bets," value investors whose trusted financial adviser has them sticking with mutual funds for the long term.

Their cultural icons include anyone who conforms to the "slow and steady wins the race" model. Finance Minister Paul Martin is the sympathetic father figure whose brand of middle-of-the-road common sense they admire. Royal Bank CEO John Cleghorn is respected for getting to the top by being prudent and playing by the rules. And if the Toronto Maple Leafs could only win the Stanley Cup, all would be right with the world. Security-seeking Ascetics love the idea that with hard work anyone can get ahead, and they are prepared to put their noses to the grindstone.

The diversity that exists within each generation of Canadians (i.e., the existence of a number of social values tribes within each of the three major cohorts) is sometimes less interesting than the strands of commonality that extend across generational lines. In each quadrant of the 3SC map, we find at least one values tribe from each of the three major generational groups in Canada. In the upper-right-hand quadrant, motivated by Financial Independence, Stability and Security, we find Rational Traditionalists (Elders), Disengaged Darwinists (Boomers) and Aimless Dependants (Gen Xers). In the upper-left-hand quadrant of our social values map, we find those who value Traditional Communities, Institutions and Social Status. Among these Canadians are the Extroverted Traditionalists of the Elder cohort, the Anxious Communitarians of the Boomer cohort and the Thrill-seeking Materialists of the Gen X cohort. Personal Control and Self-fulfillment (the dominant values in the lower-right-hand quadrant of the 3SC map) are also fundamental motivations that cross lines of age. These values are most pronounced among Cosmopolitan Modernists (Elders), Autonomous Rebels (Boomers) and Autonomous Post-materialists (Gen Xers). Finally, in the lower-left quadrant, where Experience-seeking and New Frontiers are fundamental motivations, we find Connected Enthusiasts (a Boomer tribe), New Aquarians and Social Hedonists (both Gen X tribes), and also some of the aforementioned Cosmopolitan Modernists (Elders).

Socio-Cultural Map: Positions of Tribes 1999

TRADITION

Anxious
Communitarians 6%

Aimless
Dependants 8%

Rational
Traditionalists 12%

Extroverted
Traditionalists 7%

Disengaged
Darwinists 17%

Pre-Boomers 25%

Thrill-seeking
Materialists 3%

Security-seeking
Ascetics 6%

Boomers 39%

Social
Hedonists 4%

Gen Xers 35%

Autonomous
Post-materialists
9%

Connected
Enthusiasts 6%

Cosmopolitan Modernists 6%

Autonomous
Rebels 11%

New Aquarians 5%

OTHER-DIRECTED

INNER-DIRECTED

INDIVIDUALITY

3.
The Changing Meaning of Money

As a means, I saw that money was all but absolute: it could now realize every fantasy of creation or murder. And at that moment of extreme instrumentality, it was transforming once again: into an absolute end. Money was valued not for its power to convey wishes: rather it was the goal of all wishes. Money was enthroned as the God [of] Our Times.
—James Buchan,
Frozen Desire

Our culture is focused on money as never before,
but there is more behind our orientation towards money than
the simple "fear and greed" that stockbrokers and other cynics claim constitute our basic motives. Unlike our parents and
grandparents, we see money as a complex entity, not just a
loaf of bread or the fruits of our days spent "working for the
Man." Our changing understanding of money is manifesting
itself in a range of new behaviours. We no longer put what we
have left over after paying for the essentials (i.e., food, clothing, shelter) into a low-interest savings account in a credit
union or the local branch of one of our beloved banks. Half of
us are now gambling with our money, directly or indirectly, in
the stock market. And more of us find ourselves keeping the
extra cash the waiter or salesperson gives us by mistake when
making change; increasingly, we seem to be taking our moral
instruction from the unrepentant tone of that familiar
Monopoly card: "Bank error in your favour! Collect $200!"
And when we die, knowing as the playwrights Moss Hart and
George S. Kaufman did that we can't take it with us, we are
less likely to bequeath our entire financial legacy to the
church or even to our kids. Values have changed and with
them has changed our orientation to the stuff we've been told
makes the world go round. Although the changes in our conception of currency are numerous, and in a few cases even
puzzling, this much is clear: social change is not small change
when it comes to money.

The Fathers of the Canadian Confederation were not a
bunch of free-spending, freewheeling, wild and crazy guys.
Ever look at the picture of these gentlemen assembled at the
1864 Charlottetown Conference? Or at the list of their names,
which starts with our Scottish-born first prime minister, Sir
John A. Macdonald, and includes Mackenzies, McTavishes,

McDougalls, McGregors and Browns? This was a stolid and dour lot. Of course, Sir John A. was certainly not the most uptight of the bunch. Thanks in part, surely, to the copious quantities of whisky he consumed, he may even have been a touch looser than his erstwhile Upper Canadian Grit allies, one of whom was a Bruce County MP I count among my Presbyterian ancestors, Reuben Eldridge Truax.

One of our two founding peoples were the Scots, who were the captains of the commercial empire of the St. Lawrence, headquartered for two centuries in Montreal's Golden Mile in Westmount. They ran the Hudson's Bay Company, which was the backbone of our early economy, and they established the banks that would finance our first national dream, the transcontinental Canadian Pacific Railway. These sober and prescient businessmen presided over the expansion of the Canadian economy from the private enclaves of the Mount Royal and Mount Stephen clubs for the first seven decades of the twentieth century, while the politicians in Ottawa and the provincial capitals did their bidding and balanced almost every peacetime government budget until 1974, when leaders with different values started running the show. As the University of Toronto historian Abraham Rotstein has quipped, "There was Methodism in their madness."

The other founders of Canada were the French-speaking Canadians who emigrated from Normandy and Brittany from the early 1600s until the British conquest in 1759. These too were a conservative lot, although you wouldn't know it to hear some modern-day Quebecers, who claim their ancestors were all hot-blooded Latins—as in Latin lovers. In fact, the vast majority of Quebecers are the descendants of people every bit as dour as the Scots of Montreal. They were Catholic and spoke French, but they shared conservative values with the Anglo loyalists in Montreal and Upper Canada. (It would appear that even in those days, demography was not 100 per cent of one's destiny. What sort of tribes, I wonder, would have revealed themselves had our social values tracking been available then?) Certainly, French-speaking Canadians had a lot more in common with the United Empire Loyalists and other English-speaking Canadians than they did with the wild-eyed republicans south of the border in the United States. Canada's founding peoples were counter-revolutionaries, and even our rebels were pretty cautious. Today's versions—alienated Westerners and Quebec separatists—may be upset with the status quo, but they certainly wouldn't do anything that would threaten their pensions, the value of their savings or their vacation plans.

Money, particularly in North America, has always maintained an important relationship to status and power. Sometimes that relationship has been one of virtual equivalency, and at other times it has been more complex. The evolution of this relationship has traced a long path through countless behaviours and events. Recall, for instance, the nouveaux riches of North America in the nineteenth century, who built European-style châteaux in Newport, Rhode Island, and other castles across the country. Efforts by American robber barons to emulate the lifestyles of the European aristocracy inspired our famous predecessor, Thorstein Veblen, the father of the study of modern status symbolism and the author of *The Theory of the Leisure Class*, to invent the phrase "conspicuous consumption" to describe this ostentatious display of new-found wealth. But no one captured the meaning of money in the Jazz Age better than F. Scott Fitzgerald in his 1920s classic *The Great Gatsby*, in which the narrator, Nick Carraway, observes, "The very rich . . . are different from you and me." Later this century, in the 1980s, we saw this ostentation in another incarnation when Wall Street masters of the leveraged buyout celebrated greed, and Donald Trump flaunted his wealth as the new King of Marvin Gardens in Atlantic City. And now, a decade later, we seem to be witnessing the birth of a new economy based on the development of information systems and biotechnologies that the stock market is valuing on a basis that departs dramatically from the multiple-of-earnings formula that has long been the standard for industries in the old economy.

Microsoft's Bill Gates has, it is true, built himself a nice little $100-million home on the Pacific coastline, and together with his wife, Melinda, he is starting to engage in "ostentatious philanthropy," but we are not really duplicating the 1980s decade of greed or the conspicuous consumption of the Roaring Twenties. The picture is more nuanced than that.

One of the ways socio-cultural researchers try to make sense out of social change is to view the evolution of human civilization through the lens of major belief and authority systems. Ron Inglehart, Neil Nevitte and their colleagues on the World Values Study team have developed a paradigm for the evolution of value systems that is very useful in conceptualizing social change in Canada. This paradigm was introduced in our earlier discussion of social change, and for our purposes here, as we engage in an analysis of Canadians' changing orientation towards money, it again proves a useful conceptual implement.

In general—not just in Canada—sociologists understand that traditional societies are focused on the maintenance of the status quo as enforced by patriarchal, religious and hierarchical authority. In these societies, individuals conform to social norms, customs and traditions.

Modern societies, on the other hand, are focused more on economic growth and individual freedom. Authority is based on the rule of law and the rationality of the market. Individuals shift their orientation from conformity to tradition and then again to the achievement motivation and the ostentatious display of the symbols of their success.

Postmodern societies, as a rule, presume that a certain level of economic prosperity is assured. They are post-materialist in the sense that they shift their emphasis from achievement and consumption to well-being, harmony and spiritual meaning. Individuals in postmodern societies do not defer to traditional religious and secular authorities, but rely instead on trusted intermediaries or on themselves. Traditional people put any savings they have in a bank. Modern people seek out a trusted financial adviser, who typically spreads risk among a variety of financial instruments. The postmodern early adopter gets the needed information from a variety of sources and trades investment vehicles on the Internet.

When this paradigm is applied to Environics' socio-cultural map, it is fairly evident that the tribes at the top of the map are oriented towards a combination of traditional and modern values, while those at the bottom hold a combination of modern and postmodern values. Very few Canadians are purely traditional in orientation. While it is true that many immigrants hold some values that can be construed to be traditional, even these new Canadians have, for the most part, embraced the values of personal achievement and economic prosperity. These values likely motivated them to come to Canada in the first place.

In traditional societies—those in which societal authority is vested in the state and the church—the currency that makes things happen is power. In the case of warlords, barons and monarchs, their power, though steeped in symbolism of various kinds, is fundamentally derived from their monopoly on physical force. The religious establishment, on the other hand, bases its power on its putative control over the keys to the gates of heaven. This power is, of course, rooted in another kind of force: the force of people's own need to believe in some overarching divine order and ultimate justice, particularly in the face of earthly suffering or oppression. This is how, in traditional societies, the guardians of state power and the clergy rule over peasants, who possess few rights and privileges.

In modern societies, money displaces secular and religious power as the principal medium of exchange. Over time, as manufacturing replaces agriculture as the cornerstone of the economy, the bourgeoisie join and ultimately displace the nobility and the clergy at the top of the social pyramid. Peasants move off the farm and become working proletarians in the cities. Eventually, they coalesce into labour unions and electoral blocs to demand a greater share of the national wealth. As productivity improves, they have sufficient discretionary income to become consumers and then investors and owners. Raw (i.e., physical) power is replaced by money as the asset that buys the freedom, security and happiness to which people aspire.

During the period of modernization, the average person is motivated by the need to achieve material success. At first, this means rising out of poverty, but later it entails purchasing ever more expensive symbols of success on the social hierarchy. Modernization is characterized by individual striving and material hedonism. Money displaces physical power and spiritual monopoly as society's most potent force.

Ultimately, however, the modern quest for progress and acquisition proves unsatisfying. Not only do we as humans adapt to, and hence derive diminishing satisfaction from, steadily increasing standards of living, but we begin to see our quest itself as an inherently frustrating one. As Robert J. Samuelson notes in his discussion of the phenomenon of entitlement in America at the end of the twentieth century, "By whatever label, the American Dream implies that tomorrow should be better than today. If better is the destination, then there is no arrival and there is continual frustration at the endlessness of the journey." And so, as material striving reveals itself to be only part of the answer to the personal and civil questions modern individuals and societies pose, modernity gives way to the postmodern quest for meaning.

In postmodernity, a certain level of affluence is presumed. For the most part, there is sufficient disposable income to allow average citizens to meet their basic needs as well as their need for social recognition. In the parlance of the Age of Aquarius, people have enough toys—perhaps more than enough—and they begin to aspire to experiencing the unique, the novel and the emotionally gratifying. Theirs becomes a quest for meaning. The valued currency of postmodernity, therefore, is vitality: the power not of the sword or of the pocketbook, but of one's personal energy. In postmodernity we value spontaneity, authenticity, well-being and harmony. We focus on being rather than becoming and try to live in the present while being aware of our past and

Traditional, Modern and Postmodern Society Societal Goals and Individual Values			
	Traditional	*Modern*	*Postmodern*
Core Societal Project	Survival in a steady-state economy	Maximize economic growth	Maximize subjective well-being
Individual Value	Traditional religious and communal norms	Achievement motivation	Post-materialist and postmodern values
Authority System	Traditional authority	Rational-legal authority	De-emphasis of both legal and religious authority
*Valued Currency**	Power	Money	Vitality

Source: Ronald Inglehart. Modernization and Post-modernization
* Category added: Michael Adams

cognizant of our future—both as individuals and as a civilization. In the postmodern condition, we also aspire to balance the twin and sometimes conflicting modern legacies of freedom and equality. For Baby Boomers, this quest manifests itself in their need to question everything and yet believe in something. Theirs is the search for values but not necessarily the God they were introduced to in their youth.

As you read this book, you will see elements of tradition, modernity and postmodernity in Canadians' attitudes towards money. And you will see how each of our thirteen tribes has embraced the values of tradition, modernity or postmodernity (or combinations thereof), as manifested in an emphasis on traditional patriarchal and institutional power, on money and the symbols of social success, or on personal vitality and the quest for experience and meaning.

4.
Making It

I don't like money actually,
but it quiets my nerves.
—Joe Louis,
   world heavyweight
   champion, 1937–1949

At the turn of the last century, almost half of all Canadians worked in agriculture or in a job related to agriculture. As Canada became industrialized, more and more of us were employed in resource extraction and manufacturing. Fledgling companies in these sectors grew in size and became large, hierarchical and bureaucratic. In the private sector, and then in the public, we witnessed the evolution of a new kind of worker, "the organization man" identified in William H. Whyte's famous 1956 book of that title. The organization man was, in the felicitous phrase of the management guru Peter Drucker, "a knowledge worker." He pushed paper, not product. Today we are witnessing another transformation of our economy, from one focused on the exchange of goods and services to one based on the exchange of information. And as information has been digitized, its transmission has become instantaneous: it can be sent almost anywhere on earth in a matter of a few seconds. The organization man in the bureaucracy is now being replaced by communications technology that allows information to go directly from producer to customer and from seller to buyer.

Within a period of one hundred years, we have evolved from a society in which only a few had the information (we called them the elite, and they included accredited professionals like doctors, lawyers, bankers and, in Canada, accountants) to a society in which a substantial majority of employed Canadians have become, in some sense, knowledge workers, and in which virtually everyone can be a knowledgeable consumer. These changes reflect a broader socio-cultural evolution in Western societies during recent decades: the individual has begun to replace political and economic institutions as the locus of control.

Selected Trends on the Socio-Cultural Map—Canada 1999
Making It

TRADITION

OTHER-DIRECTED

INNER-DIRECTED

Financial Concern Regarding the Future

Need for Status Recognition

Risk Aversion
Social Darwinism

Racing Against the Clock
Need for Personal Achievement

Networking

Heterarchy

Fulfillment Through Work
Reprioritizing of Money
Penchant for Risk-Taking
Reprioritizing of Work

Scepticism Towards Big Business
Pursuit of Happiness to
the Detriment of Duty

Need for Escape

Rejection of Order
Importance of Spontaneity in Daily Life

Personal Creativity
Adaptability to Complexity in Life

Need for Autonomy
Control of Destiny
Rejection of Authority

INDIVIDUALITY

But as sovereignty has devolved from institutions to people, so too has the stress of leadership. We have exchanged the relatively passive role of subjects and followers for the more active and responsible role of citizens and leaders. In the workplace, we are no longer obsequious peons in a hierarchical bureaucracy; increasingly we are self-employed entrepreneurs in a world of ever-changing networks and relationships. Indeed, one of the most remarkable expressions of individualism in our society has been the rapid growth in self-employment during the past two decades. Between 1976 and 1998, self-employment doubled in Canada, and there are now close to 2 million Canadians who call *themselves* boss. As increasingly independent workers, we no longer merely execute instructions; we spend our days exchanging information and making decisions using ever more sophisticated, mobile, integrated and interactive systems of communication.

Even those of us who continue to work in large bureaucratic organizations are demanding more autonomy and personal control. Progressive leaders are recognizing, and even encouraging, this trend. They are empowering their employees to make tactical decisions in line with corporate strategy. Front-line Air Canada employees are encouraged to upgrade their frequent flyers from coach to business class when space is available, and flight attendants go out of their way to accommodate passengers on the spot. Senior managers know that it is far better to have empowered and motivated employees who sometimes make mistakes than to have passive automatons who only follow orders and provide disgruntled customers with some silly form to fill out. In today's world, the post office is dystopia.

Proportion of Self-Employed in Workforce			
	1986	*1991*	*1996*
Males	8.7%	12.9%	15.7%
Females	3.4%	6.1%	8.8%

Source: Census data

As we discussed in the chapter on social change in Canada, we have been moving from the "status" quadrant on the socio-cultural map towards the "autonomy" quadrant. On average, when mapped according to their social values, working Canadians—both men and women—are in the autonomy quadrant. Individuals who fall into this portion of the map are generally stronger than other Canadians on values such as rejection of authority, control of destiny, rejection of order, equality of the sexes, multiculturalism and heterarchy. The workplace may well be where these values manifest themselves most clearly. The values associated with the autonomy quadrant are those of people who wish projects to be led by the person with the most interest in the subject, the person with the most competence or expertise, and the person with the most time available to do the job. The project leader's title on the organizational chart, as well as her age or seniority in the organization, is irrelevant. So are the clothes (uniform) she is wearing, the hours of the day she chooses to work and

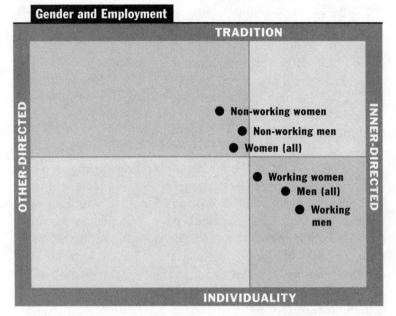

the location where she chooses to accomplish the task—in the office, at home or sitting with her laptop in Chapters or at Starbucks. As Canadian workers progress further into the autonomy quadrant of the social values map, a move facilitated in part by new technology, the conformist hierarchical bureaucracy of the 1950s will give way to the individualistic heterarchical model of the future.

If you want to know where we have been in terms of organizational structures, look at the military. It is customary in the military to begin at the bottom, as a private, and hope to work your way up to general. If you follow orders, eventually you'll be giving them. You start with no perks and no stripes, and hope to have lots of both by the time you're through. One of my favourite cartoons shows a colonel barking at a captain: "Think for yourself, Captain," to which the underling automatically responds with a stiff salute, "Yes, sir!"

Contrast this organizational model with that of a dot-com start-up where the twenty-five-year-old "propeller-head" who is writing the software that may just make everyone in the company a millionaire next year works when he wants (sometimes twenty-four hours a day), where he wants (as long as his screen connects to the server), and wears what he wants (a South Park or Rage Against the Machine T-shirt these days). His salary, like everyone else's in the company, including that of the twenty-eight-year-old marketing MBA who is the president, is relatively modest. They all have shares, though, and can't wait for the IPO (initial public offering of shares on the stock market).

Although working Canadians are embracing the freedom and independence that accompany self-employment and increasingly heterarchical organizational structures, these benefits do not come without cost. Diminished security, increased competition and a rapidly changing economic environment are combining to raise stress levels substantially among Canadian workers. With technology developing at an astonishing pace and industry racing to keep up, many Canadians are terrified that they will be left behind. Not all fear that they will actually sink into poverty, although if we keep electing governments that trim back employment insurance benefits and the social safety net, who knows who could end up panhandling on Main Street?

One theme of this book is the growing sense among Canadians that they are competing in a Darwinist jungle; this feeling of feverish and incessant competition is pushing many Canadians to their psychological limits. Or at least that's what they tell pollsters. People tell us they spend their days in a frantic pursuit of the almighty dollar, only to feel so exhausted that they have no time to stop and smell the roses. This is particularly true of parents, most of whom are in the workplace during the day, not at home with the kids.

For the majority of Canadians, I believe, complaints about overwork are the complaints of people who are trying to do too much, trying to cram three lifetimes into the one we are all accorded. Although we live, on average, about twenty years longer than our ancestors did a century ago, we are still hard-pressed to find time for all the things we want to do. As

Staffan Linder predicted in his prescient 1970 text *The Harried Leisure Class*, with increased affluence has come a more hectic lifestyle; we expect ever more of ourselves and each other, particularly in our places of work. Statistics Canada reports that the number of Canadians working extended hours (i.e., more than forty hours per week) has increased. Long hours are particularly common among the self-employed, a group that makes up a substantial proportion of the Canadian workforce, as noted earlier. How are Canadians responding to this increased workload? In 1998, Statistics Canada's *General Social Survey* reported that one-third of Canadians between the ages of twenty-five and forty-four consider themselves workaholics, and half the people in this age group say they feel trapped in a daily routine. More than half of Canadian workers are concerned that they do not spend enough time with family and friends. Even postmoderns can feel guilty about something—in this case, not living up to their own demanding standards.

Evidence shows that workplace stress can double the risk of heart attacks. The *National Public Health Survey* has found that longer hours and more job stress make workers susceptible to unhealthy lifestyle choices, including smoking, eating more fatty foods, drinking more alcohol and watching more television. Workers and employers share in this loss. Statistics Canada estimates that the annual cost of work time lost because of stress is $12 billion.

> *About one-third of Canadians really pity people who consider their work to be the be-all and end-all of life. Those most likely to pity workaholics are the idealistic New Aquarians in Generation X and the live-for-today Connected Enthusiasts in the Baby Boomer cohort.*

You may be wondering by now—or perhaps were wondering long before picking up this book—why we work so hard if all this is so bad for us. One reason is perceived necessity. The rise of dual-income families over the past few decades has had as much to do with financial need as it has with choice. Alan Mirabelli, executive director of the Vanier Institute of the Family, points out, "If you are a single breadwinner or an unattached person, your income has not kept up. In fact, it has declined. The way families have adapted to all this, when they see their real income decline, is they simply fielded another worker." "The Growing Gap," a report released by the Centre for Social Justice in Toronto, indicates that while the average Canadian corporate CEO's salary rose by 15 per cent in 1995, 11 per cent in 1996 and 13 per cent in 1997, to an average of more than $1.5 million per year, including stock options, workers' wages rose only 2 per cent during the same period, less than the rate of inflation.

Another reason for Canadians' feverish work schedules is job insecurity. Although things began to look brighter on a macro scale in the late 1990s, fully one-fifth of Canadians today feel that their jobs are threatened. There is little generational variation with respect to this phenomenon. Elders, Boomers and Gen Xers are about equally likely to feel their situation is precarious. Among the tribes, Connected Enthusiasts, the most emotional and least career-oriented of Boomers, are the ones most likely to feel that their employment status is insecure. The Cosmopolitan Modernists, the most affluent and successful tribe in their cohort, are much less likely than other Elders to feel that their employment situation is precarious.

As the economist Robert Frank points out in his book *The Winner-Take-All Society*, job insecurity, and the intense competition it breeds in the workforce, leads to longer hours and higher levels of job stress. As employees strive to distinguish themselves from one another (in the eyes of either an employer or potential clients), they may become overtaxed. Frank quotes the economist Juliet Schor: "'People who work reduced hours pay a huge penalty' in career terms. . . . 'It's taken as a negative signal' about their commitment to their employer. Thus, when relative performance is an important determinant of reward, private incentives lead people to work too much."

When Canadians see their job situations as precarious, as our research suggests many do, they are more likely to work more and worry more, and less likely to seek personal fulfillment in their work. Instead, they come to see work simply as a way to pay the bills, a grind they must endure each day if they don't want to be confronted with an even worse fate. As the social safety net continues to fray, unemployment is to be avoided more than ever—even if that means sometimes settling for the first miserable job that comes along.

Of course, not all Canadians share this apprehension about their employment status, and opinions about the nature of work and its relationship to workers' lives in general vary widely. Canadians are divided on the question of whether work is all about the money. One-half of Canadians see a job as nothing more than a paycheque, and certainly not a vehicle to achieve personal fulfillment; the other half disagree. Given that we spend half our daylight hours at work (more like three-quarters in the winter), is it not astounding that only half of us get personal satisfaction from this activity? And if this is so, think of the huge untapped potential in the Canadian workforce, potential that could be unleashed in the form of energy, commitment and productivity if more employers could figure out better ways to motivate their workers.

The conformist hierarchical bureaucracy of the 1950s is giving way to the individualistic heterarchical model of the future. Information technology is not causing this evolution in the organization of work in our society, but technology certainly is facilitating and accelerating an evolution in our socio-cultural values, values that were evident and growing long before e-mail or video conferencing. In short, technology is allowing us to do now what we have wanted to do for some time: be mobile, be independent and have control over our own schedules and workspaces.

Each generation of technology seems to have a shorter half-life than the last. Remember the magic of the fax, a technology that ruled for perhaps a decade before receiving some stiff competition from that now familiar electronic carrier pigeon, e-mail. And soon voice-recognition systems will zap the keyboard, and Dick Tracy's two-way wrist radio will be realized as a ubiquitous personal communications device connecting everyone to everyone in real time everywhere. Research in Motion's Blackberry e-mail pager is just the beginning.

As more people work from home, there will be an increased need for distinct spaces within the home for work and play, sometimes called flex housing, a trend that is causing us to add more square feet to our homes even though there are fewer of us in them.

There are virtually no generational differences on the question of work and money, but there are very significant differences *within* each generation. Among the Elders, the Cosmopolitan Modernists (the most modern and best-educated Elders) are only half as likely as the Extroverted Traditionalists to consider work just a source of income. Among the Boomers, the pattern is repeated, with the Autonomous Rebels (again the most modern tribe in the cohort, and generally the most successful) only half as likely as the Anxious Communitarians to see work as merely a source of income. Finally, among Gen Xers, most Thrill-seeking Materialists, Aimless Dependants and Social Hedonists consider work to be just a source of income, while most New Aquarians, Autonomous Post-materialists and Security-seeking Ascetics consider it a source of personal satisfaction.

It's important to keep in mind, when examining these facts, that personal fulfillment on the job is seen as desirable by almost all Canadians. The distinction is that among more traditional tribes, intrinsic satisfaction tends to be less important than income, while among more modern tribes, job satisfaction is seen as more important. Most members of the more modern tribes—whatever the generation—would not work in a job that was not personally fulfilling, in a job that did not give them lots of space for personal autonomy, or for an employer whose ethics and reputation were questionable. Employers who wish to attract such employees—and take note: even the post office and the military need to recruit these sorts of people—should be aware of the importance of ideals and individualism to members of the more modern tribes.

Just as they disagree about the importance of finding personal satisfaction in their employment, Canadians also hold diverse opinions regarding the degree to which their identity is symbolized by their employment. When they're asked how important their job is in giving meaning or direction to their lives, Boomers tend to consider it more important than the Elders or Gen Xers. But far more striking than the differences *among* the generations are the differences *within* the generations.

Among the Elders, one-third of Extroverted Traditionalists say their jobs are very important in giving meaning to their lives; less than one-fifth of Cosmopolitan Modernists feel the same way—even though virtually everyone would agree that they have "better jobs." CosMods are saying that their jobs must be meaningful, but there are other significant things in their lives. Balance in their lives is more important than the title on the office door.

Among the Boomers, more than one-third of Anxious Communitarians say their jobs are very important in giving meaning to their lives, but less than one-fifth of Autonomous Rebels share that sentiment. In general, the personal fulfillment on which Cosmopolitan Modernists and Autonomous Rebels are focused is achieved in all aspects of their lives, not just work. On the face of it, these findings are astounding and seemingly contradictory. The people with the best jobs, the best financial prospects and the highest incomes put less emphasis on the work in their lives than those who are not as advantaged. I would argue that the reason for this apparent contradiction resides in the *relative* importance of work in the lives of more affluent Canadians. Financially secure groups such as the Autonomous Rebels and the Cosmopolitan

Modernists are less interested in the rewards and achievements associated with their jobs because they are more able than others to afford the things and experiences that money can buy. Because of their affluence, they also have more time than others to appreciate the wonderful things in life that money can't buy. Personal fulfillment for these people has evolved beyond survival or the ostentatious display of the material rewards of hard work. These are also the people who no longer look to any one institution for meaning and security in their lives. A religious institution, the family, the government and their work may all be important to some degree, but the individual is the final agent and arbiter. These successful Canadians focus on well-being, harmony, enlightened hedonism and spiritual meaning.

The pattern of differences within the generations repeats itself among the young. Among Gen Xers, Thrill-seeking Materialists are four times more likely than New Aquarians to say their job is very important to their sense of direction in life. New Aquarians are much more likely to find meaning in family, friends, spirituality or activities outside of work.

My Job Is Very Important to the Meaning of My Life	
All Gen Xers	23%
Thrill-seeking Materialists	47%
Aimless Dependants	29%
Security-seeking Ascetics	23%
Autonomous Post-materialists	19%
Social Hedonists	18%
New Aquarians	11%

In all the generations, those in the upper-left quadrant, the one focused on traditional communities, institutions and social status, are more likely to define themselves, or partially define themselves, by what they do for a living. More modern Canadians, on the other hand, are focused more broadly on how they live, and have a more eclectic range of roles and identities.

Of course, we are affected by our jobs not only as individuals. In a sense, our families share in our employment experiences: our schedules, incomes, stress levels and feelings of personal fulfillment all filter into our households and our relationships. For this reason, it is instructive to consider the impact on families of the ways that Canadians are making money today. Statistics Canada—not that we needed to be told—has found that the stress that accompanies Canadians' attempts to balance family obligations with increasingly hectic work schedules is substantial. Indeed, those most likely to report severe time stress are working parents aged twenty-five to forty-four. Among this beleaguered group, 38 per cent of women and 26 per cent of men report feeling severe time stress. The gender differential in these results is largely a result of the fact that women continue to assume the bulk of unpaid domestic work and the burden of caring for children and aging parents. Statistics Canada reports that on average, working fathers aged twenty-five to forty-four spend 22.8 hours each week at unpaid work, while working mothers of the same cohort spend 34.4 hours on unremunerated labour. For this group of working parents, the two-hour average increase in paid working hours since 1992 has not diminished the amount of time they spend on unpaid work. Indeed, between 1992 and 1998, time spent on unpaid work increased for both men and women.

More than nine in ten Canadians agree that in a household where both partners are working, there is nothing wrong with the wife earning more than the husband. Extroverted Traditionalists are the ones most likely to see something wrong with this scenario, and Autonomous Rebels, Cosmopolitan Modernists and New Aquarians are the least likely to see any problem.

As noted earlier, a dual-income household is certainly no guarantee of wealth. Indeed, many working parents do not earn enough to hire a nanny or finance professional daycare for their children, and so must make do with informal day-care or other alternative supervision. These arrangements, which often change according to the needs and schedules of the various players involved, increase logistical problems and attendant stresses. And then, of course, parents are forced to reckon with both their guilt over leaving their children during the day and their concerns about the quality of whatever daycare arrangements they have managed to piece together. The roads of our cities are filled with stressed-out working moms and dads holding a steering wheel in one hand and a cellphone in the other in a vain effort to balance the demands of work, home and—if they're lucky—a social life.

> - *A 1997 Statistics Canada survey found that the number of telecommuters—that is, workers who perform some or all of their job from home—grew from 6 per cent to 9 per cent of the workforce in the preceding three years, bringing the total number of telecommuters in Canada to one million.*
> - *In a poll released by the employment Web site monster.ca, 38 per cent of respondents reported that the opportunity to telecommute would affect their job choice.*
> - *A survey released by Ekos in 1998 revealed that 33 per cent of respondents, if given the choice between telecommuting and taking a 10 per cent increase in their salary, would choose to telecommute.*
>
> *Reported in the* National Post Business Magazine, *May 2000*

Although their incomes are more crucial to the families they support, parents are not always the only workers in a household; often adolescents obtain part-time employment in order to partially support themselves, augment their entertainment budgets or, more rarely, contribute to the general family coffers. A large majority of Canadians think teenagers should get part-time jobs while still in school to learn to be responsible, learn how to manage money or be able to buy the things they want. However, most Canadians do not think they should get part-time jobs in order to contribute economically to their families.

What is interesting about this fact is that the main divisions are not along generational lines, but according to social values. Among the Elders, the Rational Traditionalists and the Extroverted Traditionalists are more likely than average to say that teenagers should get part-time jobs to contribute to their families; the Cosmopolitan Modernists tend to disagree with this. Among the Boomers, the Anxious Communitarians are the most likely to say teenagers should contribute economically to their families, while the Autonomous Rebels are the ones who most disagree. And among the Gen Xers, the three more traditional tribes are likely to say teenagers should work to contribute economically to their families, and the three more modern tribes are likely to disagree. The more modern tribes in each generation recognize, perhaps more than anyone, the importance of an education for the future of their children, and they are not pressuring their kids to contribute economically to the family at such a young age —especially not to a family that is already well off. This freedom is certainly a boon for the children of affluent parents—after all, Statistics Canada reports that one-quarter of fifteen- to twenty-four-year-olds say they already feel trapped in a daily routine. With tuition fees rising and a post-secondary degree becoming an ever more important credential, many adolescents will be forced to help finance the investment in their own future success.

Employers aren't the only ones who dole out cash to worthy recipients; parents have their own domestic payroll. Most Canadians agree that children should receive some sort of regular stipend from their parents, but the reasons for this, as the table on page 96 illustrates, are varied. The highest proportion of Canadians say that children should receive an allowance in order to learn money-management skills. These Canadians see an allowance as a way of teaching

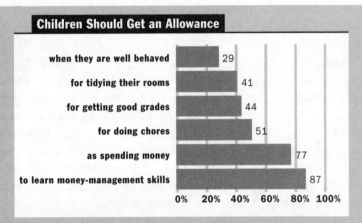

Children Should Get an Allowance

when they are well behaved	29
for tidying their rooms	41
for getting good grades	44
for doing chores	51
as spending money	77
to learn money-management skills	87

0%   20%   40%   60%   80%   100%

children about the value and role of money in our society—a lesson the kids will have to learn one way or another.

More than three-quarters of Canadians think children deserve spending money that they are free to use as they please (within limits, of course). A slim majority of Canadians think children should receive an allowance for doing chores.

Only a minority of Canadians believe children deserve a financial reward for getting good grades, cleaning their bedrooms or being well behaved. Presumably these respondents think that these behaviours should be the norm, not paid occupations. After all, Mom and Dad don't get paid for obeying the law.

Most young people are pretty optimistic about their future; their parents and grandparents are the ones who worry they won't make it. We no longer ask our young men to go off to fight in foreign wars or relegate our young women to lives dictated by biological determinism. But we do ask them to pass muster on their own in a world in which abundant employment opportunities and a generous social safety net are being replaced by cutthroat competition, a world of winners and losers. Older Canadians are beginning to worry about the consequences for those who don't come out on top in this brave new world. What are the prospects for an Aimless Dependant in the third millennium, especially when the institutions of the family, the state, the church and civil society are less able or willing to help him up when he falls?

The link between the shift in Canadian social values and significant changes in the workplace is striking. As Canadian workers have grown more committed to personal autonomy and the values of the lower-right-hand quadrant (such as heterarchy, rejection of authority and control of destiny), they have come to embrace ways of earning money that allow them the most freedom and control, such as self-employment and employment in small heterarchical businesses. Although Canadians are devoting more time to their work than ever before, they increasingly desire certain rewards in return, including the freedom to dress as they wish, take breaks when they wish, take regular vacations and work independently in the manner they find most comfortable. Even as Canadians relinquish some control of their lives by submitting to longer hours in the face of what they see as fierce competition in the workforce, they are becoming less willing to compromise on certain qualitative facets of their work experience, such as autonomy and flexibility. Some Canadians feel uncertain about the security of their employment situations, and they fear unemployment as they witness the decay of the social safety net. They recognize too, however, that their working hours make up a substantial portion of their daily lives, and increasingly they insist that their experience in the workplace afford them some measure of autonomy and independence.

5.
Spending It

Of the two—the vote and the
money—it was the money, I
[admit], that seemed infinitely
the more important.
　—Virginia Woolf,
　　A Room of One's Own

It is customary to think of modernity as having begun in the late eighteenth century with the advent of popular sovereignty and democractic rights that resulted from the American and French revolutions. The goal of these revolutions, and of the more gradual reforms in England, was to expand the political and economic liberty enjoyed by the citizens of those countries. As industrial capitalism evolved in the late nineteenth and early twentieth centuries, there was more public focus on issues of social justice for those citizens as workers. These issues were addressed violently in Russia, but gradually and more peacefully in Britain, France, the United States and Canada. By the middle of the twentieth century, a version of the welfare state had evolved in every modern country, and that development, together with the increasing productivity of Western economies, left average citizens with something few of them had possessed before: discretionary income. The economist John Kenneth Galbraith was able to ponder *The Affluent Society* in his 1958 bestseller, and the sociologist Vance Packard was inspired to extend Thorstein Veblen's insights on the conspicuous consumption of the American nouveaux riches at the turn of the century to the status-seeking American middle class of the 1950s.

Thus, the individual citizen and worker also took on the role of consumer, and the story of the latter half of the twentieth century can be seen in terms of the gradual decline in the importance we attach to our status as citizens and the gradual increase in the importance we attach to our status as consumers—consumers of goods, services, entertainment, travel, culture and an almost infinite variety of mood-altering substances. The evolution of the worker into the share-owning capitalist investor, a subject on which we will focus in chapter 6, has been just as important. Now yet another trend seems

Selected Trends on the Socio-Cultural Map—Canada 1999
Spending It

TRADITION

OTHER-DIRECTED | **INNER-DIRECTED**

Ostentatious Consumption   Confidence in Big Business
Advertising as Stimulus
Meaning of Life=Material Possessions
Concern for Appearance
Need for Status Recognition   Utilitarian Consumerism
Joy of Consumption
Confidence in Advertising
        Importance of Brand
Confidence in Small Business   Importance of Price

Deconsumption

Strategic Consumption
Enthusiasm for Consumption
Consumptivity   Scepticism Towards Small Business
Ecological Consumption   Ethical Consumerism
Discriminating Consumerism

                                     Scepticism Towards Big Business

Importance of Aesthetics

                                     Importance of Spontaneity in Daily Life

INDIVIDUALITY

ready to emerge: the most idealistic of our citizens, the New Aquarians, are agitating for a conception of the individual in North American society that transcends the cyclical and limited sphere of consumption to assume greater moral and spiritual content.

This developing trend would likely be music to the ears of Robert Frank, who points out in his book *Luxury Fever* that in the world of consumption, the adaptability that is part of our natural human endowment is less a blessing than a curse. Although our material standard of living may rise consistently, Frank explains, we so quickly become accustomed to our new toys and indulgences that we can't help demanding (and spending) ever more in order to satisfy our consumer cravings. Frank notes that some things we enjoy, such as leisure time and low levels of stress, provide lasting benefits that far exceed the temporary thrills we derive from consumption. He, like the New Aquarians, reasons, "The observation that we adapt more fully to some stimuli [such as new cars] than to others [such as time with our families] opens the door to the possibility that moving resources from one category to another [that is, spending more time doing things we love and less time earning money to buy *stuff*] might yield lasting changes in human well-being." In this statement, Frank is painting a portrait of utopian postmodernity.

Despite the cogency of Frank's argument, and nascent anti-consumerist rumblings among the early adopters of social values in the Generation X cohort, consumption among the general population is feverish. Never before in the history of our civilization have more people consumed more things and experiences with enthusiasm. The consumer is now king in our culture, a condition that disgusts elitists, moralists and the idealistic New Aquarians. We are all now consumers in the global village. And my industry (market research)—together with allied industries such as advertising, marketing and public relations—is dedicated to measuring, tracking and exploiting all our hopes, dreams and aspirations on behalf of the producers of a bewildering array of products and services, many of which we don't yet know we want. Galbraith argued in *The Affluent Society* that "if production creates the wants it seeks to satisfy, or if the wants emerge *pari passu* with the production, then the urgency of the wants can no longer be used to defend the urgency of the production."

When Canadians are asked to compare their current spending habits with their habits a year ago, a strong generational pattern emerges: the Elders are the least likely (about one in seven) to say that they are spending more, and Gen Xers are the most likely (about one in three) to report that their consumption has increased. The Boomers as a group are somewhere in between.

This generational pattern is to some extent attributable to life stage. The Elders, having already established themselves, have bought most of the material goods they require to live a comfortable life. The Gen Xers, on the other hand, many of whom have only recently left home, still have a lot of major purchases to make (home furnishings, cars, even—yes, for many the dreaded time has come—respectable clothes to wear to the office) as they begin to assemble their own homes and lives.

> *The average Canadian household spends $112 weekly on food, and more than a quarter of that is spent in restaurants.*
>
> Source: *"Why We Buy,"* Report on Business Magazine, *January 2000*

The Security-seeking Ascetics are a notable exception within their generation. Because they are more focused on future comfort and stability than on immediate gratification, they are by far the most likely members of their age group to say they are now spending *less* than they were one year ago. Security-seeking Ascetics are also the Gen X tribe least likely to report that they are on the lookout for new things. At the other end of the spectrum lie the New Aquarians, those cutting-edge early adopters who are the most likely to say they are on the lookout for things novel. This quest for novelty, however, does not necessarily indicate an inclination towards increased consumption. Unlike their fellow denizens of the lower-left quadrant, the Social Hedonists (who are more than four times as likely as the general population to say that they have bought a product over the past few months because they want to be among the first to try it), many New Aquarians are non-consumerist or even anti-consumerist in their values, and their new ways of doing things don't always involve their Visa cards.

> *At the beginning of the twentieth century, home delivery of everything from milk to clothing to hardware was fairly common. Now, as we enter the twenty-first century, we are coming full circle: shopping on-line is making home delivery a familiar phenomenon again. The motivations for delivery have, of course, changed. Today, the growing number of two-income households (in which neither partner has time to make special shopping trips after a long workday) is making Internet commerce an increasingly popular choice.*
>
> *E-commerce can be expected to continue to grow rapidly because of the convenience it offers time-pressured people*

and those who work irregular hours. There are still some bumps in the road that will have to be overcome before e-commerce can take off fully, however. There have to be guarantees that selection is broad enough and items are in stock, and also that they will be delivered on time for a reasonable fee. Customers are looking for choice, value and immediate gratification; all of these are potential advantages of shopping on the Web.

For the time being, the avoidance of taxes is another benefit of making purchases on-line. Taxation of goods bought via e-commerce is lagging seriously behind the technology itself. As a result, many Canadians are shopping elsewhere in Canada, in the U.S. or even around the world, without paying the normal consumption taxes. Needless to say, in a country as heavily taxed as Canada, tax-free shopping is no small advantage.

The level of PC ownership in Canada is comparable to that found in the U.S., and the proportion of Internet users is equal to or even higher than that south of the border. Many Canadian companies already have successful Web sites, including Chapters, Future Shop, Indigo, Megadepot, Ticketmaster and Zellers.

Thus far, the products that Canadians are most interested in purchasing on the Web are computers, books, CDs, travel, clothing and consumer electronics. These are followed by magazines, hotel bookings, videos and event tickets. Part of the reason these purchase categories have been doing so well is that those who are wired skew younger than the general population, and hence tend to purchase more "youthful" products such as CDs.

Boomers and Gen Xers are considerably more likely than Elders to have purchased a product or service through the Internet. Interestingly, Anxious Communitarians, the most consumerist of Boomers, are the least likely among their generation to have made purchases over the Web. They adore the whole shopping experience, not just the product purchased, so for them the Web experience is just too "thin." Autonomous Rebels, on the other hand, those Boomers least focused on status and material possessions, are the most likely to have made an Internet purchase. These "pragmatic enthusiasts" don't need attention from sales clerks or the shopping experience; they just want the goods—substance over style—and they want them now.

Among the Gen Xers, New Aquarians, the tribe that likes to try any new experience, are the ones who are most likely to have already made purchases on the Web. For them, the material goods are less important than the experience of doing business on-line. Also, these young people are less fearful than others of the possible downsides of e-commerce; they're the ones who describe themselves as willing to try anything at least once.

New Aquarians' complex relationship with early adoption (i.e., their inclination to harbour the most modern social values but sometimes eschew recent fads in consumer culture) is consistent with our finding that it is not, as one might expect, the modern tribes at the bottom of the socio-cultural map that are necessarily the first to adopt new products. When we examine Canadians' responses to our questions regarding early adoption of consumer goods and services, we find that it is the Extroverted Traditionalists among the Elders, not the more modern Cosmopolitan Modernists, who are the first to try new products and services. In the Boomer cohort, the Connected Enthusiasts and the Anxious Communitarians, not the Autonomous Rebels, are the novelty-seekers. Among the youth tribes, the Social Hedonists, the Thrill-seeking Materialists and the New Aquarians lead the way. All these tribes are broadly dispersed along the vertical axis of our map: they range from the very traditional (the Extroverted Traditionalists) to the extremely postmodern (the New Aquarians). So what do they all have in common? The tribes that are inclined towards early adoption of consumer goods are in all cases the most other-directed members of their respective generations. The more traditional actually want the goods; the more modern want the experience.

> In January 2000, Report on Business Magazine *revealed that the greatest decline in personal spending in the ten-year period between 1986 and 1996 was on alcohol in bars and restaurants, which dropped 33 per cent to $191 per capita. The greatest increase was in spending on communications devices such as cellphones and the Internet, which surged 40 per cent to $1,099.*
>
> Source: "Why We Buy," Report on Business Magazine, *January 2000*

If the modern tribes aren't concerned with new products, you may be wondering, just what is it that makes them so cutting edge? The answer is that the modern tribes situated towards the bottom of the socio-cultural map share one significant characteristic: they are early adopters of both new social values and new communications technologies that connect them with those of similar values and interests around the globe. In some cases, the new attitudes and ideas adopted by the most modern social values tribes are in conflict with the latest trends in consumption. Anti-consumerism, for example, is a postmodern value; it is, of course, not surprising that people who have adopted this value, despite their sensitivity to changes and advances in our society, have in many cases failed to embrace the latest consumer goods.

The relationship between social values and consumption in Canada at the dawn of the third millennium is nothing short of fascinating. In his recent book *Money and the Meaning of Life*, Jacob Needleman, a professor of philosophy, ascribes spiritual significance to money. He claims that "the outward expenditure of mankind's energy now takes place in and through money," and he reasons that

> for anyone who seeks to understand the meaning of our human life on earth, for anyone who wishes to under-

stand the meaning of his own individual life on earth, it is imperative that one understand this movement of energy. Therefore, if one wishes to understand life, one must understand money—in this present phase of history and civilization.

Although I'm prepared to leave the metaphysical questions to Needleman and his colleagues, I could not agree more with the suggestion that the way we spend the money we earn (that is, the way we convert our labour into the food, travel, gadgets, warmth, giving and peace of mind that our friends in the world of economics have so blandly dubbed "utility") has become a monumentally important facet of the way we express ourselves and manifest our identities in this world.

Take the sport-utility vehicle (SUV), for instance. This huge, increasingly popular all-terrain wagon is taken by many to be an object of conspicuous consumption at its most brazen. Gas-guzzling (less than three kilometres to the litre, in case the peasants were curious), immense (some of the larger models are more than seven metres long; you may want to measure your garage before driving one off the lot) and extremely expensive, these rolling fortresses are about as far from understatement as you can get. But when examined in conjunction with changing social values, the growing popularity of SUVs—and the concomitant popularity of monster homes and gated communities—seems to be less about ostentation than about achieving a sense of safety in a world that is perceived by many to be a Darwinist jungle. The SUV is the Sherman tank of urban warfare, as valued by middle-class North American women as the gun is by the underclass of North American males. After all, lots of vehicles that are smaller and less physically imposing than SUVs signal wealth and status, but even in once-cocky Alberta, oil executives are trucking to work in new Suburbans, leaving the Mercedes at home to sulk resentfully under a blanket, hoping at best for a weekend spin.

Another impressive example of how our changing values are informing our spending involves the idealistic New Aquarians. This tribe's purchasing decisions respond to numerous factors outside the cost/benefit template we're taught to attend to in Economics 101, not the least of which is a consideration of the ethics of the company from which they're purchasing. Six in ten New Aquarians report that in recent months, they have bought one product over another because they knew the supplier was humane and environmentally sensitive. This finding jells perfectly with our picture of the average New Aquarian as a young person with a strong social conscience and a sense that her actions can have an impact on both her own life and the world in which she lives. By contrast, only one in ten Aimless Dependants has chosen one product over another based on the criteria listed above. This is predictable behaviour for members of a disconnected and somewhat directionless tribe who feel little faith in or affinity with the people and institutions around them.

Savvy marketers understand that despite apathy among some tribes (like the Aimless Dependants), many Canadians are making increasing efforts to consume in a way that is consistent with their values. Knowing that many socially conscious people—not only young Canadians, but also many aging Boomers—are interested in lightening the burden they place on the planet and on those less advantageously positioned in the global economy, companies such as the Body Shop have launched a trend that has been dubbed New Age Capitalism. The Body Shop, created by the British entrepreneur Anita Roddick in the 1970s, is nothing if not modern personal autonomy and environmental values in a (high-priced, reusable) bottle. Such companies attract customers by highlighting not only the quality of the products they offer, but also the conscience with which these products are supposedly created. Roddick's company, for example, places a great deal of emphasis on its environmentally sound and culturally sensitive business practices. Regardless of whether the Body Shop (and others that purport to be businesses of conscience) actually conforms to these ideals in its operations—and some have questioned this claim—the very fact that ethics *can* be used as an effective marketing tool suggests that consumers are indeed increasingly using their money to buy meaning, not just product. And if you don't think things have changed, try to name one product marketed in the 1950s on the basis of its environmental friendliness.

Ethics are not the only telling ingredient in the social values tribes' purchasing decisions. A majority of Canadians, six in ten, report that when they buy a product, the brand is very important to them. Perhaps not surprisingly, it is the more materialistic tribes that are most focused on brand. Among the Elders, three-quarters of Extroverted Traditionalists say brand is very important, but only half of Cosmopolitan Modernists say the same. The pattern repeats itself among the Boomers, with three-quarters of Anxious Communitarians saying brand is very important, but only half of Autonomous Rebels ascribing the same importance to labels. Finally, among the Gen X tribes, three-quarters of Thrill-seeking Materialists say brand is very important, but only half of New Aquarians or Security-seeking Ascetics agree. The latter tribe is, of course, materialistic, but it is so future-oriented that members have the willpower to defer their consumption till much later in life.

The other thing to note here is that while brands are important to the traditional tribes in the upper-left quadrant because of their symbolic value, they are important to tribes in other areas of the map for a host of other reasons. Some Canadians, particularly those pressed for time, see brand as a shorthand guarantee of value or quality. These consumers buy the familiar brand not necessarily to impress others, but simply for their own convenience and peace of mind.

From March to August 1999, Environics International interviewed citizens in twenty-three countries on six continents regarding corporate social responsibility. The total sample comprised 25,247 citizens worldwide; one thousand or more citizens from each country were interviewed.

- Citizens in thirteen of twenty-three countries think their country should focus more on social and environmental goals and less on economic goals in the first decade of the new millennium.

- In forming impressions of companies, people around the world focus on corporate altruism ahead of either brand reputation or financial factors.

- Contributions to charities and community projects do not nearly satisfy people's expectations of corporate social responsibility. There are ten areas of social accountability rated higher by citizens in countries on all continents.

- Fully half of those who live in the countries surveyed are paying attention to the social behaviour of companies.

- More than 20 per cent of consumers report either rewarding or punishing companies in the past year based on their perceived social performance, and almost as many again have considered doing so.

- Opinion leader analysis indicates that public pressure on companies to play broader roles in society will likely increase significantly over the next few years.

- Two in three citizens want companies to go beyond their historical role of making a profit, paying taxes, employing people and obeying all laws; they want companies to contribute to broader societal goals as well.

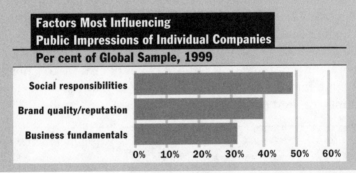

Factors Most Influencing Public Impressions of Individual Companies

Per cent of Global Sample, 1999

Of course, brands and their reputations are important to most consumers. We all want products that deliver what they promise, but what they choose to promise depends on the positioning of the marketer. Does an item promise utility, reliability, safety, aesthetics, affordability or a certain familiar symbolism? Does it purport to offer something new, innovative, cool? Automobiles, for example, have hundreds of product features and an equal array of images associated with them. Our job as social values researchers is to match product features and images with values profiles of consumer segments; this helps companies market existing products and aids in the development of new ones. For all but the most ascetic adherent to the simplicity movement, matters of utility, price, aesthetics and projected image mean a lot more than we are often prepared to admit. The New Aquarian who buys her clothes at Goodwill is just as conscious of the symbolism of her purchase as the Thrill-seeking Materialist who, in sporting the latest designer label, slavishly succumbs to the pressure exerted by her peers. The question is, Are they conforming to societal and peer pressure, or are they breaking the mould and making an effort to assert their individuality? All brands have attributes and all brands have markets. Are they mainstream or niche? Are they local or global? Are they boring or are they cool? These are the keys to the universe of consumer marketing in our era.

> *Canadians spend more of their household income on clothing than they do on any other non-food item (an average of $2,182 a year, which is roughly equal to the cost of running our homes).*
>
> Source: "Why We Buy," Report on Business Magazine, *January 2000*

In addition to our concern for the ethics and symbolism that underlie our purchases, there is another important consideration for many of us when we reach for our wallets: the speed with which we can experience that exhilarating "hit" of acquisition. We are a culture obsessed with the emotional jolts associated with immediate gratification. And when it comes to consumption, this is a trend with a distinct generational pattern: members of the youth tribes are markedly more likely than members of older generations to report that they have recently bought a product because they could have it right away.

Bought Because I Could Have It Right Away			
All Canadians	Elders	Boomers	Gen Xers
42%	38%	40%	49%

As is so often the case, there are also significant differences *within* the generations. Within each age group, members of the most consumption-oriented tribes are the ones who say they have bought something simply because they could have it right away—among the Elders, the Extroverted Traditionalists; among the Boomers, the Anxious Communitarians; and among the Gen Xers, the Social Hedonists and the Thrill-seeking Materialists. The Security-seeking Ascetics, as they often do, provide an exception within their generation: they are more likely than other members of Generation X to be willing to accept deferred gratification.

Despite the diversity of factors at play when Canadians make purchases, the proverbial bottom line remains a consideration of paramount importance. As a rule, we don't like to part with any more loonies than we absolutely must. Unlike our cousins to the south, who often spend recklessly on purchases with strong symbolic value, Canadians are constantly on the lookout for bargains; we shop and shop till it's the retailers who drop. If you want confirmation of the different spending habits of Canadians and Americans, just ask retailers in Florida, who have a hard time making Canadian snowbirds part with their money, even when they offer to take the Canadian loonie at par with the U.S. greenback.

Wal-Mart understands this Canadian penchant for bargain hunting, and the American retailing giant destroyed Eaton's, a venerable national institution, by capitalizing on our parsimony. Canadians—rich and poor—must feel they are getting a bargain or they just will not buy from you, no matter how fond their memories of your grandpa's catalogue. We always suspect that we are being ripped off—the ultimate insult to a Canadian. We all have a brother-in-law who bought exactly the same thing last week for half the price at some discount outlet, or who got it for practically nothing by cashing in his Canadian Tire money. It seems the only time you see Canadians in Toronto's fashionable Yorkville is when Holt Renfrew has a sale. The rest of the time, most luxury merchandisers have to rely on the patronage of American tourists.

In a fascinating *National Post* article, Serena French describes a shopping excursion in Florence, one of the great commercial hubs for tourists in Italy. French writes of an encounter with a nineteen-year-old Brazilian student named Bruno who was manning a booth in the San Lorenzo market. Having seen his share of tourists, Bruno remarked, "The Americans are the ones who buy the most. The Japanese buy Armani, Gucci, only expensive things." French inquired, "And the Canadians?" Bruno's answer sounds decisive: "They always want a discount."

The young Brazilian's analysis is consistent with the data Environics has amassed over the years; our polls provide ample support for the stereotype of the frugal Canadian. More than four in five Canadians report that no matter what the product, price is always very important to them. Though there is a strong consensus on this question, it is interesting to note that the more traditional tribes at the top of the sociocultural map are the most insistent that price is always important. There are a couple of likely reasons for this. One is that people with traditional values tend to be less affluent than people with modern values, so it is not surprising that they would be more focused on price. As well, they want to get the most bang for their buck. Avid consumers feel "opportunity cost" in their very bones: any dollar saved on one particular purchase can later be spent somewhere else. Members of modern tribes, those who say that "money isn't everything," tend to be the same people who say that "price isn't everything."

Consumption is an important part of Canadian culture. However, as we enter a new millennium, we are beginning for the first time to see the glimmer of a culture less enamoured of *things*. As we move from modernity to postmodernity, material objects are losing their lustre and we are beginning to relish our purchases less. Although we still spend lots of money on lots of products and services, and likely will in the future, trends such as joy of consumption and ostentatious consumption are in decline. In response to Canadians' somewhat diminished interest in consumer goods, retailers have had to attempt to produce a more experiential model of shopping to continue to engage buyers. In making this change, they are on the right track. Canadians, like good fledgling postmoderns, are becoming more interested in the sensuous and emotional experiences their money can buy and less fixated on the tangible toys that are so seductive to a modern culture.

Canadians' diminished attention to material goods and increased focus on experiential consumption has produced winners and losers, like any change in the market. The losers are, of course, those who persist in trying to hock *stuff* without offering potential buyers some emotional or sensuous inducement. These producers, sensing the cynicism and fickleness of the market at large, have begun to target younger consumers—particularly members of tribes like the Thrill-seeking Materialists—because they believe that these young people are the closest we have today to the ingenuous consumers of the 1950s. It is a popular misconception that young people, because they have been exposed to an unprecedented barrage of ads and exhortations to consumption all their lives, are particularly savvy and thus wary of promotional strategies. In fact, this is true of only the two most modern youth tribes, the New Aquarians and the Autonomous Post-materialists, plus the new Security-seeking Ascetics tribe (for different reasons). In general, young people are just as likely as anyone else to belong to P. T. Barnum's infamous band of suckers, whose numbers, we're told, increase by the minute. Thus marketers do in fact have a potential gold mine in Canadian youth, and their efforts to "get 'em while they're young" are understandable. Cable stations such as YTV (Youth Television) and Teletoon are filled with ads aimed at children as young as four and five. Consumer marketers are invading our universities, colleges, high schools and even elementary schools with all manner of exclusive deals designed to implant an indelible image of their logos on the impressionable minds of our other-directed youth. Even the reviled tobacco firms, it has been revealed, have launched stealth campaigns to lure teenagers into an early dependency on their addictive and potentially lethal product.

It is a fascinating and, in some ways, disturbing trend in our society that for many of our youth the traditional imprints of identity—gender, age, ethnicity—are being replaced by an affinity to "cool" brands of consumer products. This is the market corollary of the general shift in our culture from demography to values as prime motivators of human, and therefore consumer, behaviour. Rock b(r)ands, TV and movie stars, sports heroes and other celebrities all play a part in building and maintaining power brands in the minds of young people.

If the losers in this increasingly experiential economy are those who are still trying to sell *things*, the winners are those who are ready and willing to offer Canadians all the thrills and delights they desire—for a price. A recently released Statistics Canada report tells us that in 1998 casinos surpassed lotteries as the largest generator of non-charity gambling revenue; that year, casinos accounted for 38 per cent of gambling revenue, compared with only 1 per cent in 1992. Almost $2.8 billion was wagered in Canadian casinos in 1998. Clearly, Canadians are not just interested in spending money on a ticket that symbolizes the possibility of striking it rich: they're dressing up and heading out—and they're taking their wallets with them.

> *Canadians shop an average of five hours and fifteen minutes*
> *each week—a third more time than we spend on reading or*
> *self-education.*
>
> Source: *"Why We Buy,"* Report on Business Magazine, *January 2000*

Another recent trend we have identified is the increase in shopping as a form of escape. We don't need the stuff, and we're not sure we really want it; but we have to do something, so we shop. Part of this phenomenon can also be attributed to the fact that shopping malls have succeeded in establishing themselves as private "public spaces," natural places to meet and socialize, replacements for the town squares of yore. Going to the mall has become the default leisure activity for many people, and it is yet another manifestation of our collective move towards spending on experiences as much as on tangible products. West Edmonton Mall is the Disneyland of shopping centres; believe it or not, you can actually take a ride on an indoor submarine between bouts of shopping, and if you're too exhausted to go home at the end of the day, you can check into the Fantasyland Hotel and rest in one of its theme suites.

Our rejection of the conspicuous facets of consumption in favour of experiential consumption is one symptom of our declining concern for status symbols in the form of consumer goods. The following statistics are telling on this score:

- In 1983, 38 per cent of Canadians said that they always chose their clothes with great care. In 1999, that figure was only 26 per cent.
- In 1983, 48 per cent of us said looking good was becoming more and more important. In 1999, only 30 per cent felt the same way.
- In 1983, 35 per cent said that if they were to move, the first thing they would want of their home was for it to look good. By 1999, that number had declined to 25 per cent.

As ever, though, the broad trend of declining interest in showy purchases masks significant distinctions among the tribes. As far as conspicuous consumption is concerned, there are two Canadian values quadrants that count: the first, and most important, is the lower-right Autonomy quadrant. This is where we find two leading tribes: the Autonomous Rebels of the Baby Boomer generation (the defining segment of that generation) and the Autonomous Post-materialists of Generation X. Both of these avant-garde tribes are characterized by values such as autonomy, personal control, rejection of authority, rejection of order, equality of the sexes, heterarchy and the like. They do not embrace the values of consumption, conspicuous or otherwise. They are staunch individualists, uninterested in impressing others with cars or gadgets. Sure they want to get rich, but they don't have ostentation in mind; they're more interested in exploring their own personal capacity. Theirs is the ultimate Revenge of the Nerds in a global and competitive world.

Sharing space in the lower half of the map are two other interesting tribes: the Cosmopolitan Modernists of the Elder generation and the New Aquarians of Gen X. Neither of these tribes is interested in conspicuous consumption. As I've already noted, the New Aquarians' defining characteristic is a rejection of materialism; often they express their distaste for consumer culture by buying their clothes at second-hand outlets. The CosMods, on the other hand, are the financial winners of their generation, and they already have all the stuff they could ever want. Forget the Joneses—these Canadians are ready to stop and smell the roses. Their goal is emotional, intellectual and spiritual meaning. They are deconsuming as they sell the family home and move to smaller, more manageable quarters where they can contemplate their legacy to this planet.

The materialists are drawn from the most traditional tribes of Canadians: the Extroverted Traditionalists, the Anxious Communitarians and the Thrill-seeking Materialists. Unlike their age peers in the lower-right quadrant, these are our society's true consumers. They are not particularly successful, though; these are generally not the adaptable innovators at the vanguard of the New Economy. In many cases, these consumption-happy Canadians are drowning in debt as they chase the dream of Martha Stewart; no matter how much they spend on emulation, the lady (to say nothing of her standards) remains elusive, ever beckoning but constantly receding into the distance, trailing raffia and the scent of lavender behind her.

> By the end of 1998, there were more than 35 million credit cards in circulation in Canada, roughly double the number of just one decade earlier and four times the number of two decades earlier. Total personal debt is more than 100 per cent of annual after-tax income. And over the past decade, personal bankruptcies have tripled (from 25,817 in 1988 to 75,465 in 1998).
>
> Source: "The High Life," Report on Business Magazine, January 2000

It is interesting that we have seen evolve in the 1990s a new group of young people who have chosen to copy their more successful peers not by creating wealth, but by saving it. Because they're so busy shoring up resources for later in life, the Security-seeking Ascetics have, like their more modern counterparts, come to eschew conspicuous consumption. Members of this tribe cannot hope to score on the NASDAQ— they're too risk-averse—but they can evolve out of aimless dependence into responsible citizenship by, for example, putting money into their RRSPs before their thirtieth birthday. In the final analysis, although they embrace only a few of the modern and postmodern values of their more autonomous age peers, Security-seeking Ascetics have leapt decisively off the traditional train of conspicuous consumption.

While our research indicates that Canadians' interest in conspicuous consumption is in decline, Robert Frank points out that luxury spending in the U.S. is growing at four times the rate of spending overall. What could account for this apparent disparity between the two nations' spending habits? One reason is that Canada is moving more rapidly into post-

modernity than the U.S., which remains largely a modern culture focused on personal achievement and the ostentatious
display of status symbols. An anecdote about a Canadian
bank may suggest a further explanation. The story goes that
a certain Canadian bank did extensive analysis before
launching a "gold level" of preferred customer service at its
branches. The idea was to remodel certain branches so that
wealthy customers could enter by a separate entrance and be
serviced in a luxurious setting, avoiding the common lineup
the rest of us have to use. A consulting group was brought in,
and a few "test" branches were remodelled. The experiment
was a complete flop. No one used the service. The bank went
back to the consulting firm and asked why. It turns out that
the consultants had had no values data for Canada, and so
they had used American data instead. (After all, Canadians
are basically the same as Americans, right?)

The service was a smash hit in the States, where people
thought being wealthy entitled them to such an obvious display of privilege. The rich thought it was only proper, and
the less-than-wealthy expected it (likely dreaming that one
day they too might make it onto the cushy carpet in the rear
section of the bank). Wealthy Canadian customers, on the
other hand, preferred to keep their wealth a non-issue in
public. They did not want to show off. The "gold" customers
avoided the fancy door and service and stood in line with the
rest of us.

Of course, the super-rich have accountants who do their
banking, but in general the wealthy Canadian does not want
to stand out publicly—a lesson this particular bank learned
after spending hundreds of thousands of dollars on remodel-
ling. In general, global marketers know they must be sensitive to Quebec's distinct society, but they often assume to their
detriment that the rest of Canada is indistinguishable from
the United States. In some ways, there is a convergence of
values, but many differences between the two populations
remain, and some of the disparities between them are actually
growing. A nuanced understanding of the similarities and

differences in the two nations' cultural attitudes towards wealth can make all the difference in the cutthroat world of consumer marketing.

6.
Saving It and Investing It

I knew when I was getting stock tips from my shoeshine boy it was time to get out of the market.
—Joseph Kennedy, 1928

At the turn of the last century, the average Canadian had very little in the way of savings. Most people spent almost everything they earned on food, clothing and shelter. The social safety net was the family, and it was not uncommon to find two, three and sometimes four generations living in the same home. That was the case not only on the farm but also in the large Victorian houses we still see standing in our towns and cities.

As ties and obligations among family members receded, and the devastation of the Depression was felt, the state took a larger and larger role in providing cradle-to-grave social security to protect people from the ravages of ill health, unemployment and old age. The goal was to eliminate poverty and destitution, and by the 1970s we had nearly succeeded. The state spent or redistributed half our national income, and Canada had become one of the best countries in the world, if not *the* best, expressed in the quality of life of the average citizen. The motivator for the broadening of the role of the state was the harmonious confluence of idealism and self-interest. The two world wars and the Depression made everyone aware that there were frightening forces at large—the alien ideologies of fascism and communism and the pernicious boom/bust cycles of market capitalism not least among them—against which individuals were powerless to protect themselves. We turned to the state to protect us, first from expansionist ideologies, and then from the financial vulnerability that can accompany senescence or unforeseen misfortune.

What we wanted for ourselves, we also wanted for our fellow citizens. In Canada, our self-interest was matched by a noble sense of Christian duty to others; it is no accident that the Canadian welfare state was built by Liberals but inspired by the idealism of Canada's early social democrats. The CCF

Selected Trends on the Socio-Cultural Map—Canada 1999
Saving It

TRADITION

Saving on Principle
Financial Concern Regarding the Future

Aversion to Complexity in Life
Risk Aversion

Legacy

Confidence in Government

Deconsumption

OTHER-DIRECTED

INNER-DIRECTED

Reprioritizing of Money
Penchant for Risk-Taking

Pursuit of Happiness to
the Detriment of Duty

Control of Destiny

INDIVIDUALITY

and later the NDP proposed; the Liberals and occasionally the Tories implemented.

Expo 67 may well have been the culmination of the idealism that had been taking shape during the preceding decades. Individual Canadians felt good about themselves, confident in their leaders and supportive of governments that wished to build a humane, compassionate and thriving nation.

Unfortunately, we all bit off more than we could chew. During the 1970s oil crisis, governments spent more than the economy could support, so we borrowed for current consumption and mortgaged our future. The chickens came home to roost in the 1980s and 1990s, when a quarter of our national income was needed to pay the interest on our accumulated debt.

By the 1990s, we were getting only seventy-five cents' worth of services for every dollar we were paying in taxes, some of which were wrested from us by the new and detested tax on goods and services, the GST. Governments were forced to cut back on some of the generous social programs they had implemented, most notably health care and employment insurance. Not surprisingly, Canadians lost confidence in their governments and their leaders as services eroded, and we began to think that we would have to take much greater responsibility for the social security we had come to see as the responsibility of the state. Earlier governments encouraged this trend towards financial independence among citizens by starting a program of registered retirement savings. This tax-deferral scheme encouraged Canadians to take money from their current income and invest it for future use, either in retirement or in the event of a financial emergency. This plan fundamentally changed the way Canadians save.

In the 1950s, whatever savings Canadians had were safely deposited in their interest-bearing savings account in their credit union or at the local branch of one of the major banks. More affluent people bought bonds issued by the government. A small percentage of Canadians, usually the wealthiest, owned shares of publicly traded companies listed on the stock exchange. Conservative investors bought Bell Canada and Imperial Oil; risk-takers bought penny mining stocks, hoping their bets would turn into a bonanza. Over the past forty years, however, an increasing proportion of Canadians have bought riskier investments that have promised higher yields than those of a savings account or bonds issued from Canada's treasury.

The government encourages Canadians to invest in the stock market by allowing them to defer the capital gains tax on these investments until the funds are taken out of the market. At that time (presumably either on a rainy day or upon retirement) one's income will supposedly be lower, and therefore so will one's marginal rate of taxation. Today, nearly half of Canadians own publicly traded stocks, either as direct shareholders in companies like BCE and Nortel or indirectly through mutual funds, an increase from only one in five in the mid-1980s. Investors can buy and sell stocks themselves over

Percentage of Canadians Who Own Shares or Mutual Funds

Year	Percentage
1983	13
1986	18
1989	23
1996	37
2000	49

Source: TSE data reported in The Globe and Mail

the Internet, or they can rely on the advice of financial advisers who themselves can be bankers, stockbrokers, insurance agents, accountants or self-educated experts.

Have reduced government spending and efforts to encourage Canadians to provide for their own financial futures been successful in checking the tax-and-spend trend, which had begun to spin out of control? At the turn of the millennium, Canadians seem relatively content with the balance between the taxes they pay for public services and the money that is left in their pockets at the end of the day. In "selling" the existing tax scheme to us, governments now appeal almost solely to our self-interest: they highlight the value of universal health care, high-quality public education and a sound social safety net, not only for those who make use of these services, but also for the well-being and security of our society as a whole. Most of us understand that it's safer and healthier to live in a society where people are provided for on some basic level than it is to live in a Darwinist jungle. The idealism we knew in the 1960s and 1970s is all but forgotten by most Canadians today—

although the hopeful and altruistic world-view of the New Aquarians, the quintessential early adopters, may be a harbinger of a return to more utopian thinking.

But before we assume that Canadians have it all figured out and are paragons of fiscal restraint, let's look at some numbers. Despite the fact that almost a third of us have RRSPs, the overall savings rate has declined from 12.5 per cent in 1977 to only 1.5 per cent in 1998. Consumer savings in Canada are at a forty-year low.

Some economists feel that this does not represent a problem. Martin Coiteux, associate professor at the École des hautes études commerciales in Montreal, suggests that because of the gains Canadians have been earning on their investments in the stock markets, they are in fact saving nearly 20 per cent of their total incomes. In recent years, capital gains have come to dominate investor income, replacing both interest and dividend earnings.

This shift in Canadians' investment practices reflects a long-term change in our attitudes—from "a penny saved is a penny earned" to "a penny gambled is a potential nickel"—in our 3SC social values scheme, that is, from saving on principle to a penchant for risk-taking, and perhaps even more strikingly, from deferred gratification to immediate gratification. After all, incremental gains garnered in secure, long-term savings schemes can never provide the same exhilarating hit as a well-timed and profitable move on the NASDAQ—even if the latter also presents the possibility of loss.

There are a few telling shifts taking place in the world of Canadian investment, however. In 1998, both contributors and contributions to RRSPs declined for the first time since 1991. About 29 per cent of tax filers (6,122,000 people) contributed to an RRSP during the 1998 tax year, down 0.6 per cent from the previous year. They contributed $26.6 billion, down 3.8 per cent from 1997 after adjusting for inflation. In total, Canadians contributed only 11 per cent of their allowable limit. These declines occurred despite an increase in employment income during the year.

Canadians with higher incomes tend to contribute the most to their RRSPs. This is not surprising; of course those with more disposable income are able to sock away more money for retirement than those who require the money they are earning simply to subsist. This, combined with the fact that fewer than one-third of tax filers contribute to RRSPs, has prompted some critics to lambaste the program, calling it a subsidy to wealthier members of society. Jim Stanford, the economist for the Canadian Auto Workers union, remarks, "Ironically, the richer you are, the bigger the tax subsidy. High-income investors actually get a higher subsidy than your average schmuck." He observes that the RRSP program costs governments $18 billion a year in forgone taxes, making it "one of Canada's most expensive social programs."

However, attacking the RRSP system is, in socio-cultural terms, like spitting into the wind. One aspect of growing individualism is that people want to take their destiny into their own hands, and RRSPs speak strongly to this motivation and to others associated with personal autonomy. If we look at broader trends in RRSP use, we see that these plans are in fact becoming more popular. Between 1988 and 1998, the number of taxpayers increased from 16.7 million to 20.9 million—up 25 per cent. During the same time frame, the number of RRSP contributors grew from 3.7 million to 6.1 million, up 65 per cent, and the contributions made more than doubled, from $12.2 billion to $26.6 billion.

In addition to optional RRSPs, there are of course the obligatory savings plans for Canadians—namely, the Canada Pension Plan and the Quebec Pension Plan. Both of these schemes address a desire to have one's life and financial affairs managed by a large institutional authority—a declining aspiration in our culture. It is perhaps not surprising that Canadians' inclination to leave their finances in the hands of others is diminishing, because today, unlike in the past, those who allow others to make their decisions for them are beginning to feel ripped off. Malcolm Hamilton, an actuary at William M. Mercer, points out that the young are the ones whose interests are most compromised by the CPP. In 2003, when the contribution rate rises to 9.9 per cent of earnings up to $37,200, workers will be paying 10 per cent for a benefit that ultimately will pay out 5 per cent. Hamilton emphasizes that "it's really the young who would be better off without it. Those over 45 would be silly to drop it." Many Canadians are losing confidence in these collective saving schemes and are beginning to think they could do better on their own. For a time, Canadians were turning to mutual funds, but now they are demanding even more independence and autonomy. More and more, citizens are participating directly in the stock market and monitoring their own investments.

In the 1980s and 1990s, risk-averse investors who wished for better yields but didn't want to bet on individual stocks flocked in droves to mutual funds. These funds pulled together a number of stocks (often focused on an industry sector or a regional market) into one portfolio; they supposedly represented a new mode of investing that was more profitable than traditional savings accounts or bonds but less risky than individual stocks. These funds seemed the answer to the average Canadian investor's prayers in the final decades of the twentieth century, and by the end of the 1990s more than 40 per cent of Canadian households owned mutual funds.

In June 2000, The Globe and Mail reported, "In about three months, Canadians will be able to register on StockGift.com, a U.S.-based Internet service that allows brides- and grooms-to-be to tell their guests which stocks they want as gifts. Guests visit the Web site, choose a gift, and send the company money to buy the stocks." What could be a more prominent signpost of our changing orientation towards money? Yesterday we registered for china to match Grandma's Wedgwood pattern; today we register to have friends and relatives beef up our portfolios. This service would have been unthinkable forty years ago.

However, Canadians' drive for personal autonomy and control over their own financial affairs was not to end with the mutual fund. In fact, fund sales plunged 50 per cent in 1999, to $17.7 billion from $35.4 billion just a year earlier. This decline is partly a result of high consumer spending and lower RRSP contributions overall. But this phenomenon can also be attributed in part to the fact that even mutual funds require more mediation than many Canadians are willing to accept. As we become more wired and gain more access to financial information, we feel increasingly capable of making our own decisions and managing our own portfolios. And if we hadn't already been inclined to orchestrate and monitor our own investments, the fact that most large mutual funds did not even match the performance of the Toronto Stock Exchange index may well have sufficiently diminished our faith in fund managers anyway.

If mutual funds are the investment vehicle of choice for fewer Canadians, where are we beginning to put our money? Directly into the stock market, of course. As our desire for autonomy increases, and our faith in paternalistic institutions wanes, the stock market is emerging as the ideal arena for Canadians to use their own resources (both fiscal and intellectual) to further their own ends, without placing trust in governments or financial gurus.

Discussing an analogous trend in the U.S., an article in *The Economist* pointed out that "growing trust in Wall Street has been accompanied by falling trust in other institutions, such as the media and government. These phenomena are probably connected. Americans have lost their faith in people who claim to promote the public interest, believing that their fine words are empty. Meanwhile, they have warmed to people who are efficient, but who make no claim to lofty motives."

In 1998, 48.8 per cent of Americans owned stock, compared with just 40.4 per cent as recently as 1995. And stocks now account for more than half of Americans' financial holdings, up from 40 per cent in 1995. Of course, this is not a strictly American phenomenon. North of the border, we can expect direct investment by individuals in the stock market to continue to climb. Canadians' growing individualism and wariness of large institutions means not only that they are becoming less likely to entrust their financial futures to government but also that they are less likely to want their investments mediated by stockbrokers and fund managers. As people gain access to more and more information and technology, they will desire (and realize they can exercise competently) greater control over their own financial destinies.

Increased individual financial autonomy involves both increased rewards and increased risks, and risk-aversion is a key factor in a person's decision to assume greater control over her own financial affairs. Perhaps the least risk-averse of Canadians in this respect are the Cosmopolitan Modernists. CosMods are the least likely of all Canadians to report that they need their money in the short term and therefore don't want to take financial risks. Next in line in terms of absence of immediate financial need are the Security-seeking Ascetics of Generation X. In the case of this younger tribe, however, their secure state of affairs does not translate into diminished risk-aversion. The Security-seeking Ascetics are saving scrupulously, and they're not taking any chances. They may not need all their money right away, but when they finally loosen up and allow themselves to enjoy it later in life, they're counting on it being where they left it.

In general, despite the prosperity Canada is enjoying at present, there is still a great deal of anxiety on a personal level when average Canadians consider their long-term financial futures. This anxiety is among the features that have contributed to the coalescing of the Security-seeking Ascetic tribe. When two-thirds of Canadians say they are very concerned that they will not have enough money to live comfortably in the future, it is hardly surprising that a segment of the young population has become determined to begin securing its future financial well-being today. The Security-seeking Ascetics are no longer depending on the institutions their grandparents trusted implicitly; these young Canadians are starting to save seriously in anticipation of the day that the public pensions finally go bankrupt.

The Baby Boomers are even more concerned than the Gen Xers about their financial future. To some extent this concern can be attributed to life stage—how many of us are worry-free as we contemplate the day when we cease to earn and start to live solely on the avails of our productive years?—but some tribes have good reason to be concerned. The Connected Enthusiasts are particularly overwrought, and justifiably so. These are the fun-loving Boomers who refused to grow old—a stance that in its less mature form can be a refusal to grow up. While it may be cool to be spending money on cool new experiences and a cool youthful lifestyle as they do, there is nothing particularly cool about having the financial situation of a young person once you have reached middle age. "Live for today" is a great motto—until tomorrow arrives. The Connected Enthusiasts, more than any other Boomer tribe, can now see the less-than-comforting writing on the fiscal wall, and they're getting worried.

The Boomers' collective history and their social values inform their investment decisions in interesting ways. They are perhaps the most age-denying generation in history. They worship youth—their own youth—with a remarkable generational egocentrism. They have a great sense of generational exceptionalism, and they see themselves as markedly different from, and superior to, previous generations. After all, they experienced the revolution in social values that transformed our society forever, starting (but certainly not ending) with the rejection of religious, patriarchal and hierarchical authority.

If in the 1960s their motto was "Don't trust anyone over thirty," and in the 1970s it became "Don't trust Nixon," after that it seemed that Boomers just wouldn't trust anyone. This is a mental posture the Gen Xers, too, seem to have taken to heart, which is one of the reasons why *The Simpsons,* a cynical but still lighthearted show, is their favourite family sitcom.

Baby Boomers, like most people, need financial advice. But because of their values and life experience, they are less likely than members of previous generations to put blind faith in financial advisers. They are more inclined than their parents to shop around for financial products and ideas, to have several sources of advice and to show no reluctance to abandon an adviser who is unhelpful or failing to stay ahead of the game. In many cases, Boomers eschew the idea of a personal financial adviser altogether.

The Internet certainly is providing astute investors with the option of buying and selling stocks and other financial instruments on their own. However, I suspect that the more important trend in financial services—and a similar trend is afoot in the area of personal health—is not "disintermediation," but rather a search for new, trusted intermediaries. When it comes to money and health, the trend, as indicated by our socio-cultural research, is to consult many sources of information, not just one, and establish serial relationships with experts and professionals, rather than making a lifelong commitment to one.

We cannot all be fully expert on every aspect of our lives. However much we desire personal control, we will always have to exercise it in a world of expanding interdependence. In the future, each of us will have one or two areas in which we are the experts in our circle of friends and colleagues and in which we are looked to for advice (e.g., the best wines, the best travel destinations, the best bargains, the best movies, the best herbal remedies), but in other areas of our lives, we will of necessity require the advice of others. Daddy and the government won't always be there for us, and even the formerly trusted doctor, lawyer, accountant or financial adviser may not always have the best advice. We'll find our own solutions to our own problems, getting by with a little help from our friends.

7.
Giving It Away

Mankind was my business. The common welfare was my business; charity, mercy, forbearance, benevolence were all my business. The dealings of my trade were but a drop of water in the comprehensive ocean of my business!
    —Jacob Marley's ghost,
        A Christmas Carol

One of the most striking trends in Canadian philan-
thropy in recent years—and one that is intimately linked to the
changes in social values that have been discussed throughout
this book—is the move towards donor-directed charitable giving. "Donor-directed giving" is the term ascribed to the phenomenon of individuals and organizations demanding
involvement in, and control over, the allocation of the funds
they donate to charity. More and more charitable organizations are giving donors the opportunity to offer funds to specific projects or initiatives, and thus to see the concrete results
of their contributions. "Here are the computers your donation
purchased, Ms. Ahmed"; or, "Mr. Costa, this is the garden
your firm helped to restore"; or, "Mme Bouchard, these are the
young people being given a second chance to build self-
esteem, thanks to your support for our summer leadership
camp." Donor-directed giving is a highly instructive example
of the way changes in values that are not overtly fiscal can
affect Canadians' orientation towards their money and the
uses to which it is put. Canadians' interest in shaping their
charitable giving is strongly rooted in their increased desire for
personal control and autonomy, their diminished willingness to
surrender control of their affairs to impersonal or bureaucratic
institutions and their refusal to donate merely out of a sense of
guilt, duty or noblesse oblige.

The spring 2000 issue of *Philanthropic Trends*, published
by Ketchum Canada, includes a section entitled "What
Individual Donors Are Looking For." The article focuses on
the desire of potential donors to control their own charitable
contributions and reports that in the era of donor-directed giving, potential donors increasingly

- insist on earmarking gifts for specific purposes, rather
  than simply leaving the gift designation to the charity;

Selected Trends on the Socio-Cultural Map—Canada 1999
Giving It Away

TRADITION

OTHER-DIRECTED

Meaning of Life=Material Possessions
Awareness of Mortality
Need for Status Recognition

Legacy

Confidence in Government
Meaning of Life=Family

Social Darwinism

INNER-DIRECTED

Community Involvement

New Social Responsibility   Global Ecological Awareness

Importance of Spontaneity in Daily Life
Need for Autonomy

INDIVIDUALITY

- turn to issues-focused philanthropy, especially causes involving community betterment;
- make revocable gifts and take advantage of giving vehicles that meet personal financial-planning needs, such as flexible endowments;
- seek long-term relationships with organizations that offer meaningful opportunities beyond the commitment of financial support; and
- insist on long-term planning and regular reporting of tangible results beyond the bottom line.

In recent years, charitable organizations have been adopting the marketing strategies of private business in an attempt to reach potential donors. The efforts of non-profit-sector workers to have their organizations keep pace with the rate of change have included the launch of eCharity, which allows potential donors to explore charitable organizations and receive Internet updates on the impact of their contributions.

> *Richard Ivey, chairman of the Livingston Group and the Richard Ivey Foundation, has begun to harness the potential of on-line charitable giving by launching charity.ca, a Web site whose aim is to provide a comprehensive listing of Canadian charitable organizations in a format that allows potential donors to easily access causes they care most about. Two of the primary benefits of Web-based giving are a potential for personalized updates and "marketing," and greater efficiency for those who wish to give but do not have time to do extensive and time-consuming research on the groups to which they're considering directing their funds.*
>
> Source: The Globe and Mail, *May 31, 2000*

In an article published in *The Globe and Mail* in May 2000, Anne Golden and Aubrey Baillie, respectively the president and the chair of the board of trustees of the United Way of Greater Toronto, discuss the trend of donor-directed giving. They note, "Targeted giving is a natural outgrowth of empowerment trends, disillusionment with institutions, and technology that lets people access information directly and receive instant responses." The two also register a concern, however, that donors' insistence on control over their givings may diminish the autonomy and efficacy of the charitable organizations' operations. In their view, donor-directed giving engenders "a less justifiable distribution of charitable dollars, a reduced ability to protect a sustainable system of services, and an erosion of community philanthropy. When donors align themselves with the most attractive cause values can get skewed." In other words, if every donor wants to have his name on the plaque outside the gleaming new Centre for Studies in Attractive Children Interacting with Intriguing Cutting-Edge Technology, then less glamorous causes, not to mention the inglorious but essential organizational infrastructure needed to maintain them, are unlikely to receive the funding they require. Baillie and Golden prescribe a tempering of the trend towards donor-directed giving and a renewed

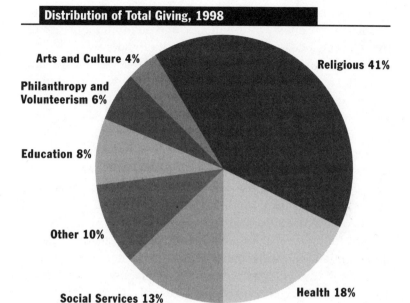

Distribution of Total Giving, 1998

Arts and Culture 4%

Religious 41%

Philanthropy and
Volunteerism 6%

Education 8%

Other 10%

Social Services 13%

Health 18%

Source: NSGVP, CCP, CCBP, Ketchum estimates

commitment to what they call collective citizenship. These changes would entail a willingness to contribute to charitable organizations simply for the common good—with no personal or promotional strings attached.

In looking at *how* Canadians have been meting out their charitable contributions in recent years, we have found evidence to support the idea that Canadians' social values have played a strong role in determining their philanthropic behaviour. Let us now turn to an examination of other facets of the world of philanthropy: who is giving money to charitable organizations, how much these people are giving and which groups and causes are the beneficiaries of their munificence.

At one time, the organizations to which Canadians gave their money were limited in number and character, and the two most obvious were the Catholic Church and the Anglican Church. As the social values of Canadians have fragmented, however, so too have the destinations of their charitable dollars. Canadians are setting their philanthropic sights on umbrella charities like the United Way, human-rights organizations like Amnesty International, and environmental groups like Greenpeace and the World Wildlife Fund.

Despite this growing secularization, however, most charitable donations in this country still find their way to religious institutions of some description. In 1998, according to Ketchum's *Philanthropic Trends*, religious organizations received by far the highest proportion of charitable donations, 41 per cent. Eighteen per cent was directed to health organizations, 13 per cent to social-service organizations and 8 per cent to educational causes. Six per cent went to organizations associated with philanthropy and volunteerism, and 4 per cent went to organizations and projects associated with arts and culture. "Other" causes, including environmental and international initiatives, received 10 per cent of all charitable givings.

Though the greatest proportion of monetary charitable donations is given to religious organizations, Environics research suggests a higher proportion of Canadian donors contribute time or money to secular organizations. In other words, although religious organizations receive more dollars on the whole, more individual Canadians are offering time or money to charities without religious affiliations, as the table below illustrates.

Strikingly, six in ten Canadians report that they have contributed either money or time to a charity related to a disease,

Have Donated Time or Money to Organization in the Past Twelve Months	
Charity related to a disease, illness or medical condition	60%
Non-religious charity devoted to social issues	41%
Church/mosque/temple	38%
Charity with a religious affiliation	26%
School or university (alumni donors)	18%
Non-religious charity devoted to environmental issues	12%
Non-religious charity devoted to human-rights issues	12%
Another charity	45%

Source: 1999 3SC

illness or medical condition in the past year. These contributions could include actions as simple as buying a red ribbon to
support AIDS research or as significant as full-time volunteering. There is a strong age pattern in this category: the Elders
(74 per cent) are more likely to contribute to a medical charity
than are the Boomers (64 per cent) or the Gen Xers (45 per
cent). Those most likely to have contributed to a medical
charity are the Cosmopolitan Modernists, and those least
likely are the Aimless Dependants and Social Hedonists.

In the case of the Cosmopolitan Modernists, support for
medical charities represents a combination of enlightened self-
interest in battles against cancer, Parkinson's disease and
Alzheimer's disease and gratitude for medical miracles already
performed on themselves, their children or their grandchildren.

The Cosmopolitan Modernists are also among those most
likely to have recently contributed money to an educational
institution. Because they're more affluent than many of their
age peers, the CosMods are more likely to have attended private schools and post-secondary institutions that are making
sophisticated efforts to keep in touch with their alumni.
CosMods desire to give something back to the educational
institutions they credit with providing the foundation for their
successful careers. These donors from the Elder cohort are the
backbone of the remarkably successful fund-raising efforts
of several Canadian universities, led by the University of
Toronto, whose UofT Campaign has raised $450 million from
its alumni over the past five years and aims to raise a total of
$575 million by 2002.

Organized religion did well when it could credibly promise
everlasting life (or threaten eternal damnation). Now it's the
health charities that promise or threaten. Every week, it seems
another medical charity direct-mails or "telemarkets" us with
an appeal for more dollars that will be directed to cures for
AIDS, heart disease, ALS, kidney disease, MS and a number of
killer cancers (breast, prostate, leukemia). The list is endless.

How do the people who are vying for scarce dollars for
these worthy causes in a highly competitive arena attempt to

garner our support? They appeal to our strategic self-interest, of course. "Donate now and increase the chances that a cure will be found by the time one of these illnesses afflicts you or someone you care about," the pitch goes. And make no mistake, the competition is fierce. I recently received a letter complaining that prostate cancer research was underfunded when compared with breast cancer research (which may or may not be true). This concern echoed the earlier cry of advocates on the other side of the gender fence that all the focus on AIDS research was deflecting attention from women's health issues.

How have the hooks charities are using changed? Well, for one thing, when the primary recipient of our charitable givings was a religious establishment, no creative pitch was needed. To a great extent, noblesse oblige and a sense of duty motivated our charitable giving. We often acted out of a desire for reward in the afterlife or—more likely—a yen to avoid a fiery punishment after death. Additionally, in the past we were more conformist and other-directed. We did things like attend church every Sunday and drop our envelope into the collection plate because everyone else did, and we faced embarrassment if we did not participate in the rituals of our community. Today we are more likely to question rather than conform, and our choices are dictated more by personal choice than by social convention. Another change affecting the solicitation of charitable dollars has been a shift in the Canadian moral universe: we have progressed from a black-and-white world of ethical rights and wrongs (complete with good guys and bad guys) to an era of ethical relativism, with as many moral codes as there are people and as many exceptions to the rules as there are circumstances in which the rules interfere with our self-interest. It is simply no longer enough to ask people to do something because it is objectively good, or to do battle with something else because it is objectively bad; if Canadians are going to contribute to a cause, they need to know *why* it's worthwhile and, increasingly, what's in it for them.

Among the most interesting forms of charitable giving in history were the plenary indulgences offered by the Roman Catholic Church. Catholic doctrine dictates that a sinner's efforts to address his sin must be twofold: he must seek forgiveness through confession, and he must undergo a certain punishment for the commission of the sin. Even after having been forgiven by God, the Church has proclaimed, the sinner still has a certain debt of punishment to pay in purgatory before his soul can be considered cleansed and worthy of heaven. Enter the plenary indulgence, which at various points in history has been purchased with dollars or deeds, and which serves as a sort of "get out of jail free" card. An indulgence can lop time off one's unpleasant tenure in purgatory and speed one's way to heaven. Plenary indulgences were first offered by Pope Urban II in 1095 in order to induce young men to volunteer to join in the First Crusade. Over the years, indulgences were granted for generous donations to cathedrals and universities. The German Dominican friar Johan Tetzel, in his efforts to raise funds using the plenary indulgences, marketed them with this catchy couplet: "As soon as the coin in the coffer rings, the soul from purgatory springs." In the late sixteenth century, Pope Pius V declared that the Church would cease to issue indulgences as rewards for charitable givings, but plenary indulgences are still issued for other pious acts to this day.

Sources: Winnipeg Free Press, *December 1999;*
The Globe and Mail, *September 1999*

If in the past charitable giving was motivated by traditional values—chiefly deference to institutional (in this case, religious) authority—in the future philanthropy will be motivated by postmodern values: autonomy, hedonism, harmony and a quest for personal spiritual meaning. Giving will often be spontaneous and even self-interested. It will take on new forms, as it has in the case of credit-card companies that offer opportunities for convenient philanthropy through cards that allocate money from each purchase to the cause of the cardholder's choice (e.g., her alma mater, Amnesty International, gay-rights advocacy groups). And just as consumption has begun to lose some of its conspicuousness as we move through modernity and into postmodernity, the current wave of ostentatious munificence will give way to more understated forms of charitable giving.

In addition to self-interest and rational (as opposed to fear-induced) altruism, another prime motivator of Canadians' charitable donations is the knowledge that, as the saying goes, you can't take it with you. Environics asked Canadians to agree or disagree with the statement that one of their goals is to leave as much money as possible to others, such as children, other family members or chosen charitable organizations. There are interesting generational differences on this question, but perhaps the most fascinating differences arise *within* the generations. In many cases, members of tribes in the same age group give vastly different answers.

To contemporary Canadians, it's obvious that you can't take it with you, and this is one simple and fundamental motivation for charitable giving. However, even this seemingly self-evident truth has not always been accepted. For example, ancient Egyptian pharaohs would actually know more opulence in the afterlife than they did during their relatively short reigns on this humble earth.

Generally, a pharaoh's body would be laid in a chamber with a few of his most personal possessions. Additional valuables would be placed in more distant chambers, as would immense stores of provisions, including food and wine. Periodically, fresh provisions would be brought to the tomb as offerings meant to sustain the erstwhile leader as he wandered in the afterlife. Sometimes the pharaoh's cattle would be slaughtered at the time of his death so they could accompany him. In the later dynasties, some pharaohs' servants would voluntarily ingest poison after the demise of their masters. They would then be buried outside the walls of the pharaohs' burial chambers so they could continue their service in the hereafter.

During their lifetimes, ancient Egyptian monarchs lived in dwellings far inferior to their tombs. Indeed, even the most exalted figures were often housed in buildings that were extremely humble compared with the pyramids where they were ultimately laid to rest. Egyptians reasoned that although the house of a living person could be repaired or rebuilt during that person's lifetime, a pharaoh's final resting place—the pyramids were also known as "castles of eternity"—would need to endure, quite literally, forever.

Rather than deferring gratification until later in this life, the Egyptians deferred their gratification until the afterlife. The historical payment for indulgences by the Catholic Church followed a similar logic. Even the largest donation was a pittance when measured against eternity.

As tempted as we moderns may be to scoff at such practices or find them quaint, vestiges remain even in our own culture. To this day, most Canadians end up lying for all eternity in boxes made of valuable woods and lined with silk or satin sheets, beds more expensive than any they enjoyed while they were living. All dressed up with no place to go.

It is not surprising that the Elders, who are closer to death than the rest of us, are more focused than other generations on leaving an estate. But what is striking, if not surprising, is that the Boomers, despite being older, are less interested in leaving an estate than are the Gen Xers. In this respect, the Boomers truly live up to their reputation as the most self-absorbed of the three cohorts: this is a "me" generation if ever there was one.

Naturally, not all Boomers (or Elders, or Gen Xers) are alike. In each generation, it is members of the more other-directed social tribes who are interested in leaving something to others after their death: the Extroverted Traditionalists among the Elders, the Connected Enthusiasts and Anxious Communitarians among the Boomers and the Thrill-seeking Materialists among the Gen Xers.

Although not as other-directed as the Extroverted Traditionalists (and therefore not as involved in the outward appearance of status and affluence), the Cosmopolitan Modernists are concerned with the mark they will leave on this planet. Their relative prosperity and concern for community will cause many CosMods to leave significant legacies—both material and personal—to their families and chosen causes. The CosMods made it in the 1960s, 1970s and 1980s, their kids have been launched and these Elders are starting to contemplate the future. They are not neglecting the prospect of their own remaining years—they certainly want to live a long and interesting life on this earth, regardless of what's on the other side of the great metaphysical curtain—but they do want to make a difference and be remembered for having contributed something genuinely valuable to their families and communities, and they have the resources and the will to do so.

Some of the very wealthy are worried not about leaving too little to their children, but about leaving too much. Many of these people started with little or nothing, and they succeeded by doing well at school and working hard. They want their children and their grandchildren to be motivated by the same values they think account for their own success. They are willing to "invest" in their adult children and be generous to them, but they realize that if they are too indulgent, they will undermine the very values they wish to leave as their legacy. Some are setting up family foundations not only as a tax shelter but as enduring institutions that subsequent generations will use to invest in the community and in causes the family cares about.

> *More than four-fifths of Canadians say they always leave a tip when eating at a restaurant, and only 1 per cent say they never do. This is one of the very few instances where there is little generational or tribal variation on a question relating to money; apparently, Canadians across the country see it as very bad form not to leave a server something "extra" for his or her trouble, although poor performance is undoubtedly rewarded at a lower level.*

The successful Baby Boomers in the Autonomous Rebel tribe also want to make a difference, but they are even less oriented to recognition and more focused on self-interest than the Cosmopolitan Modernists. They are also less grateful to elite institutions such as universities and arts organizations than their modern counterparts in the Elder cohort. Consequently, the focus of their giving will increasingly be on cures for diseases that could potentially interfere with the hedonistic lives they wish to pursue during their final decades.

Boomer self-interest may be one reason why medical charities are among those leading the non-profit sector in revenues. Even those charitable organizations that are receiving only a modest piece of the philanthropic pie, however, are likely still doing as well as or better than they were in the past because the pie is larger than ever: charitable contributions in Canada reached a new peak in 1998 at about $5.82 billion.

Philanthropy is big business in the U.S., where Microsoft's Bill Gates and his wife, Melinda, are leading the way. They've established a new foundation—the richest in the world—and it's capitalized at $21 billion. Canada's tycoons are not nearly as munificent as their U.S. counterparts, but the average Canadian is surprisingly generous when we consider the extent to which we have institutionalized our generosity—that is, the amount we're taxed.

In the U.S., an extensive survey conducted in January 2000 among a sample of 1,985 American adults revealed that only 41 per cent of those polled said they would be willing to pay fifty dollars a month more in taxes to provide health insurance for those currently uninsured. The program, sponsored by PBS's NewsHour and the Kaiser Family Foundation, noted that 44 million Americans (18 per cent of those under the age of sixty-five) did not have health insurance in 1998—and that number is rising.

Those numbers exhibit an attitude substantially different from that of Canadians, who take great pride in a health-care system they see as equitable and humane. Canadians'

> *protectiveness of their universal medicare system has recently manifested itself in the ardent national debate over the Alberta government's determination to allow private health-care providers to offer a range of procedures that had previously been offered only by public practitioners, a move that some see as the first step towards privatization and, ultimately, the stratification of medicare. We may individually be writing smaller cheques to charitable organizations than our U.S. counterparts, but the case can certainly be made that we in fact live in a nation where philanthropy is compulsory (through taxes), rather than capricious.*

Are Canadians becoming more generous? Possibly. It is likely that growth in charitable givings can be attributed at least in part to the period of economic prosperity we have enjoyed since the mid-1990s. But the rich and the upper middle class are not the only ones who are opening their wallets for worthy causes. In 1998, a consortium of seven philanthropic organizations released the *National Survey of Giving, Volunteering and Participating* (NSGVP). This report revealed that almost nine in ten Canadians over the age of fifteen made some sort of donation to charity during the preceding year, either financially or through in-kind gifts. Clearly, it is not only those with mounds of disposable income to spare who are giving to charity; remarkably, nearly everyone in Canada is contributing in some way. The NSGVP found another striking bit of data: although Canadians with higher incomes donate more to charity in absolute terms, Canadians with lower household incomes generally contribute a greater *proportion* of their income.

One explanation for the relative generosity of Canadians of low and modest incomes is that in giving to charity, they are acknowledging how fortunate they are in comparison with others. In spite of their own modest means—say, a pension or a fixed income—they are able to spare a few dollars to help the (even) less fortunate in their own communities or in other

Percentage of Household Income Spent on Financial Donations in Canada by Level of Household Income

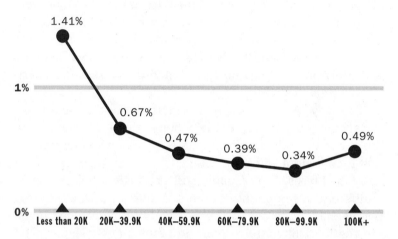

parts of the world. It's as if they're thinking, There but for the grace of God go I. Their generosity confirms in their own minds their status as people who may not be rich, but who are better off than most on this planet. More affluent Canadians, on the other hand, compare themselves not with the destitute of the world, but with their privileged peers. Their motivation for giving is far more linked to perceived self-interest than to the implicit expression of gratitude for not being destitute.

Also interesting to note is that contributions from individuals make up the vast majority of Canadian non-profit organizations' revenues. In 1998, more than three-quarters of the money donated to charity came from individual contributors, while less than one-quarter came from corporations. Moreover, corporate philanthropy is on the decline as businesses brace themselves for integration into the global economy. To remain viable in the years to come, companies are opting to focus more on fundamental business practices and less on their countries of origin.

How do the contributions of individual Canadians break down among the social values tribes? Once again, social values and financial behaviours show themselves to be closely related. For example, of the almost 50 per cent of Canadians who say they have contributed to a non-religious charity devoted to social issues during the past year, more come from the largely traditional and community-minded Elders cohort than from either of the other cohorts. However, among the Gen Xers, the idealistic New Aquarians are an exception, with fully one-half having contributed to social-issues charities over the past year.

The New Aquarians are also more likely than any other social values tribe to report that when they see panhandlers in the street, they always or sometimes give them money, an act that is consistent with their interest in effecting change on an individual basis. The Disengaged Darwinists, who are largely indifferent to the plight of others, assuming as they do that people make their own proverbial beds and must lie in them, are the least likely to respond to panhandlers. This is a bit ironic, considering that future panhandlers are most likely to come from this tribe and from the Aimless Dependants in the youth cohort.

John Stackhouse's controversial feature on homelessness, published in *The Globe and Mail* around Christmas in 1999 (the piece was topical enough to win Stackhouse a National Newspaper Award in May 2000), also offers some anecdotal insight into the behaviour of Canadians—or at least Torontonians—towards those less fortunate, whose numbers in our major cities seem to be growing at an alarming rate. Stackhouse spent seven days on the streets of Toronto, sleeping in shelters or outdoors, eating in soup kitchens and church basements, and panhandling. Stackhouse observed, "Day after day, I've noticed women giving money and food at the rate of, I'd guess, 10 for every man. Only women stop to ask me how I am; only men tell me derisively to get a job." At the conclusion of the series, Stackhouse wrote, "I was surprised by the enormous public compassion and desire to see that no one in our society live this way." Who were the people stopping out of concern to speak with the down-and-out-looking journalist or to offer him a sandwich? Probably some Cosmopolitan Modernists, a number of New Aquarians and a few Autonomous Rebels. I'd put money on the fact that those who offered disparaging remarks were Disengaged Darwinists or Rational Traditionalists: after all, *they* work hard for a living; why should they foot the bill for this guy to sit around all day?

In addition to being the ones most likely to have recently offered money to panhandlers, New Aquarians are most likely to have contributed to an environmental charity such as Greenpeace; one-third of New Aquarians report having given time, money or both to an environmental cause during the preceding year. Interestingly, New Aquarians are also the most likely of all Canadians to have donated money to a school or university they attended. This is a somewhat surprising fact, considering these young Canadians' life stage. What is more predictable is that the Cosmopolitan Modernists are the Elder tribe most likely to have contributed money to an educational institution they attended. After all, they are arguably the Canadians in their generation who have benefited most from their education, since many of them received post-secondary schooling at a time when a much smaller proportion of the population was well educated. But the New Aquarians have had substantially less time during which to generate personal revenue than the Cosmopolitan Modernists have. So what's the story? Apparently, New Aquarian idealism is strong enough to compel these Gen Xers to generosity, even in the face of fledgling bank balances. Cosmopolitan Modernists may be giving back to a system they feel has served them well, but New Aquarians are doing that and more: they're investing in the future—their future employees, their future children, their ailing planet. The ways that New Aquarians have chosen to manifest their generosity are distinctly postmodern: education and the environment are two highly future-oriented causes. New Aquarians are focused not just on their own future or the future of their immediate families, as the Security-seeking Ascetics may be, but on the future of the entire planet and as many of its inhabitants as they can reach.

Although New Aquarians may lead the way in contributing to educational and environmental causes, Cosmopolitan Modernists are most likely to be offering time or money to a charitable organization with some religious affiliation. About a fifth of Canadians report having made some sort of contribution to such a group. At the opposite end of the spectrum from the generous and community-minded Cosmopolitan Modernists are the notoriously secular Autonomous Post-materialists of Generation X, very few of whom are inclined to offer anything to religious charities.

Just over one-third of Canadians have contributed money or time to a church, a synagogue or a mosque in the past year. Predictably, Elders are the most likely to have made such a contribution, followed by Boomers and Gen Xers. Among Boomers, the Connected Enthusiasts are the least likely to have made such a contribution. Although this tends to be a tribe deeply concerned with the spiritual, its members seek spiritual fulfillment outside of traditional religious institutions. Among Gen Xers, the ever-anomalous Security-seeking Ascetics are the most likely to have contributed to a religious institution.

Canadians' charitable donations are in step with their evolving social values. Older Canadians are more interested in religious charities, while younger Canadians—at least those who have any propensity for involvement in traditional communities—are oriented more towards global causes such as environmental work and human-rights advocacy. If we feel concerned about the moral character of our youth, we would do well to keep in mind that although the NSGVP reported that Canadians over the age of forty-five contributed six out of every ten dollars that went to charity in 1997, it also found that the youth volunteer rate nearly doubled between 1987 and 1997. In 1997, one in three Canadians aged fifteen to

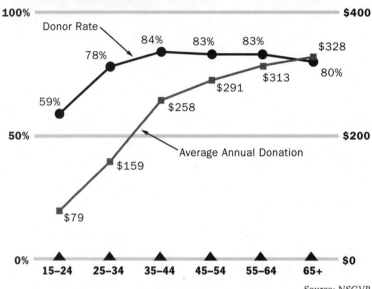

Percentage of the Canadian Population Making Donations and Average Annual Donation by Age Group

100% — $400

Donor Rate

84%   83%   83%

78%

$328

80%

59%

$313

$291

$258

50% — $200

Average Annual Donation

$159

$79

0% — $0

15–24   25–34   35–44   45–54   55–64   65+

Source: NSGVP

twenty-four volunteered for a charitable or non-profit organization. Charitable giving is changing, and although youth are less interested in Christian charity and religious organizations than their parents or grandparents are, many—particularly members of tribes such as the New Aquarians and the Autonomous Post-materialists—are looking for new ways in which to do their part, and they are finding valuable future-directed activities towards which to direct their efforts and financial support.

8.

Finding It, Stealing It and Paying Taxes

It is dire poverty indeed when
a man is so malnourished and
fatigued that he won't stoop to
pick up a penny.
—Annie Dillard,
Pilgrim at Tinker Creek

In 1997, *Reader's Digest* placed wallets containing fifty dollars each in various public places around the country to see what ordinary Canadians would do when they found them. Many tried to return the wallets (complete with the money inside) to their owners, some took the money and returned the identification, but lots of Canadians took the wallets and sauntered away, never to be heard from again by the organizers of this fact-finding mission. Toronto was the least honest site tested: for six in ten wallets it was "finders keepers, losers weepers." Moncton, New Brunswick, was the most honest Canadian urban centre: all ten of the wallets planted in that city were returned. In general, younger people were less likely to return the wallets than older people. Overall, Canadians returned 64 per cent of the wallets they found.

What reasoning would the people who happened upon and kept these unlikely wallets have employed? What does the fact that such a significant proportion of the wallets were not returned say about the values of Canadians? How inclined are we to rip off strangers? Neighbours? Friends? To what extent are we willing to prosecute our own self-interest at the expense of those around us?

If there is any country in the world where everyone has an equal chance of getting ahead in life, it would surely seem to be Canada. Unlike Europe where to some extent the family-as-destiny model still persists, or the United States where economic life often takes on the aspect of a lottery with a few spectacular winners but also many losers, Canada would seem to be the place where most people can start their lives from a reasonably secure middle-class platform, and from which they can expect a reasonably secure middle-class future. In Canada, we pride ourselves on our mindfulness of

Selected Trends on the Socio-Cultural Map—Canada 1999
Finding It, Stealing It and Paying Taxes

TRADITION

OTHER-DIRECTED

INNER-DIRECTED

Confidence in Big Business

Aimlessness
Social Darwinism

Confidence in Government

Confidence in Small Business

Everyday Ethics

Scepticism Towards Big Business
Pursuit of Happiness to the Detriment
of Duty
Rejection of Order

New Social Responsibility

Rejection of Authority

INDIVIDUALITY

the diversity in our society and on our efforts to create a level playing field for all citizens, regardless of ethnicity or cultural heritage. Witness the spectacular success of Canadians of Chinese descent, first in our educational institutions and then in the workforce. Although no society on earth is perfect in this respect, and the proverbial playing field invariably (unfortunately) yields advantages to some that others do not enjoy, on the whole those among us with an entrepreneurial spirit, an adaptability to change and a willingness to take risks can expect to be financially rewarded in the Canadian marketplace.

The only thing wrong with the Pollyanna portrait I just painted is that many Canadians appear not to believe it. They don't think we have a level playing field at all. When asked to agree or disagree with the statement that people get what they deserve, more than half (57 per cent) of Canadians disagree. When asked whether rewards and punishments are fairly given, only 37 per cent of Canadians report that they think so. And when asked whether people who meet with misfortune bring it on themselves, an overwhelming 79 per cent of Canadians disagreed. So do we see ourselves as living in a society where rewards are arbitrary, punishments are unjust, suffering is random, and we'd better take what we can when the opportunity presents itself? Should we pocket that wallet, assuming that whoever has lost it would do the same to us if given the chance?

Certainly some Canadians, particularly cynics like the Disengaged Darwinists, are inclined to see things this way. But there is other information to support the idea that there *is* some order and reason to the way things unfold in this country. When asked whether Canada is basically a fair place, 78 per cent of respondents replied in the affirmative. Although this would appear to conflict with the numbers above, the data in fact fit together quite logically when the questions are examined closely. When we see people suffering needlessly or undeservedly, we think (or at least 79 per cent of us do), "This is unfair." This sense of unmerited suffering may be aroused by anything from illness to death to a major financial setback or environmental catastrophe, and it is this sense that likely causes so many people to respond as they do to the questions in the last paragraph. However, when we think about the mechanisms we as a society have created (such as our justice system, our social-welfare system, our immigration system), we believe (or at least 78 per cent of us do) that the way things work is basically just. In short, although the cosmos may not always mete out rewards and punishments in a way that is palatable to our consciences and sensibilities, we think, to the extent that we as individuals and as communities in Canada can control things, we're doing a pretty good job.

Of course, there are huge variations in terms of our understanding of the reason and ethics that reside in the actions of others. From the perspective of Canadians (many of them in the oldest cohort) with traditional Judeo-Christian values, ethics are in precipitous decline. A sense of duty (to the Ten Commandments and the golden rule), noblesse oblige, charity, guilt, even civility have all been discarded as anachronistic notions from a bygone era. These Canadians, nostalgic for a time that may not ever have existed in the way they imagine it, have much superficial and anecdotal evidence to support the dim view they take of the moral character of our country. But as we shall see, a more nuanced reading of the moral behaviour of Canadians with respect to their money yields a picture of a society in transition. Tradition no longer has a monopoly on morality.

From the perspective of more traditional Canadians, the moral maxim since Richard Nixon resigned seems often to have been not "don't do it" but "don't get caught"—everybody does it, don't they? One-half of Canadians say that when they have the chance, they prefer to pay cash or to trade goods or services in order to avoid the GST. Environics has gathered data on the likely behaviour of Canadians in other such tests of everyday ethics, and has found that many are willing to try to "beat the system" in any way they can—even if that means cheating the government, an insurance company or another private business.

Our social values survey respondents were presented with a hypothetical situation. You have taken some guests out to a restaurant, and have had a bad meal experience. When the bill arrives, you notice that the waiter has undercharged you by forgetting to include your bar order. Do you bring the error to the server's attention or slip out quietly, accepting the unintended discount as a little gift from Bacchus? Four in ten Canadians say they would quietly pay the bill and leave. Six in ten say they would point out the error to the waiter.

There is a strong generational pattern in the responses to "the diner's dilemma": the Elders are the ones most likely to point out the error, the Boomers are less likely and Gen Xers are less likely still to own up. There is every reason to believe that this is not just a life stage phenomenon—after all, the elderly aren't any less interested in a little extra legal tender than younger people are—but rather one manifestation of a significant shift in Canadians' everyday ethics. Many older

Canadians would no doubt hold that this shift signals a decline in the moral standards of the nation.

The Cosmopolitan Modernists and the Extroverted Traditionalists, who have always won by following the rules (many of which they themselves have made), are the ones most likely to point out the error to the waiter. And though the young are much less likely to point it out, there are huge differences within the Generation X cohort. Most Thrill-seeking Materialists, New Aquarians and Security-seeking Ascetics say they would draw the waiter's attention to the oversight; most Social Hedonists, Aimless Dependants and Autonomous Post-materialists say they would not. Once again, the nuances in the behaviours and world-views of the Gen Xers are apparent; although almost none of the youth tribes (likely only the Security-seeking Ascetics) would be motivated by a traditional deference to authority or fear of reprisal in the event that they transgressed some externally imposed code of conduct, it would nonetheless appear that many young people have found their own reasons for adhering to some personal moral scheme.

What about other serendipitous circumstances? We asked respondents to imagine that the government had sent them a cheque by mistake. Would they commit the obvious sin of omission and accept the money, or would they inform our fearless leaders of the error and return the unexpected windfall? More than one-third of Canadians say they would not inform the government of such an error, and would instead keep the money. Generational differences similar to those that emerged on the restaurant question present themselves here, as the table below illustrates.

Keep Money from Government			
All Canadians	Elders	Boomers	Gen Xers
35%	21%	31%	48%

Many would justify taking money from the government by pointing to what they see as less worthy causes (than their own pocketbooks) to which government funds are allocated: subsidies and government contracts for companies located in politically sensitive regions of the country, job-creation grants for those lucky enough to live in ridings of strategic importance to the governing party, not to mention the millions and millions of squandered and ill-spent public dollars identified in the auditor general's annual report. And besides, wouldn't stealing from the government only be the equivalent of Jack (of "Jack and the Beanstalk" fame) stealing from the giant who had himself stolen the golden goose? We would be stealing only our own money or money that had previously been stolen from us (our province, region or people), n'est-ce pas?

But what about when money is not ours in any sense? Is it just government, or are there other institutions Canadians are ready to rip off if given the chance? As it turns out, the same proportion of Canadians, about one-third, say that if their bank made an error in their favour, they would not draw it to the institution's attention. Once again, the Elders are the ones most likely to point out the error, and Gen Xers are most likely to keep their mouths shut and take advantage of it. And yet again, the rather straitlaced—or traditionally moral—Security-seeking Ascetics are the only youth tribe that is more likely than average to point out the error.

Keep Money from Bank			
All Canadians	*Elders*	*Boomers*	*Gen Xers*
34%	22%	33%	44%

Under the heading of "biting the hand that feeds you," a slightly smaller proportion of Canadians, just under three in ten, say that if they mistakenly received a higher amount than usual (or deserved) on their paycheque, they would keep it. On this question as well, as age decreases there is a move away from an honest, good-faith relationship with institutions to a more opportunistic, individualistic and even dog-eat-dog mentality.

Keep Extra Money from Paycheque			
All Canadians	Elders	Boomers	Gen Xers
27%	13%	24%	41%

In the Gen X cohort, more than half of the Social Hedonists would keep the money, but less than one-quarter of the Security-seeking Ascetics would. If you want honest young employees, you couldn't do better than to hire members of the latter tribe. And it would probably be best to stay away from the party animals anyway, except when planning the company Christmas extravaganza.

Despite the widespread and growing acceptance among Canadians of cheating institutions when given the opportunity, we are still loath to rip off, or even potentially rip off, other individuals. Fewer than one in five Canadians say it's okay to keep the money if a cashier gives you extra change. People are aware that in many circumstances it is the cashier, who's likely poorly paid in the first place, who will have to make up for any such errors. Although affirmative responses to this question are lower across the board, the generational differential observed in earlier questions persists here, as younger respondents show themselves to be more opportunistic and less conscientious than their elders.

Keep Money from Cashier			
All Canadians	Elders	Boomers	Gen Xers
17%	7%	14%	29%

All the transgressions I have catalogued thus far are sins of omission—a matter of failing to point out an error made in one's favour—rather than sins of commission. Are Canadians willing to go one step further and actively defraud an institution?

An alarmingly high proportion, almost one in five, say yes. If they had the opportunity to put in a false claim to their insurance company, 15 per cent of Canadians say they would—a figure that is sure to alarm those in the insurance industry and confirm their worst fears. As with the other questions posed, the young, who feel much less attached to institutions, are much more likely to countenance or collude in this kind of fraud.

Would Make False Claim			
All Canadians	*Elders*	*Boomers*	*Gen Xers*
15%	8%	14%	23%

The Social Hedonists, not surprisingly, are the most likely to say they would defraud their insurance company: more than one-third say they would make a false claim if they could. However, the Security-seeking Ascetics, whose entire lives are structured as a giant insurance policy, abhor the idea, and fewer than one in ten would engage in such fraud.

Despite the apparent open season on many institutions, Canadians remain very honest when it comes to companies with which individuals identify more closely (as opposed to those that seem faceless). Only 2 per cent of Canadians think it is okay to steal from your employer if you believe you are underpaid. Of course, those 2 per cent matter, and companies

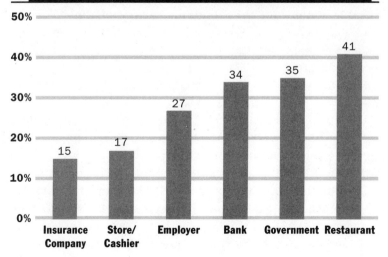

Percentage of Canadians Willing to Cheat Various Institutions

must guard against them. But the overwhelming majority of Canadians, in every one of our thirteen social values tribes, *disagree* with active embezzlement. Although some of us may think it's acceptable to pocket a little extra pay one month— that is, someone else's data-entry error is my night out—most of us would condemn deliberately skimming company funds. If you don't like your job, these respondents reason, you don't start dipping into the office cookie jar—you quit and move on.

Having a miserly boss or an unpleasant employment situation is one thing, but when it comes to matters of genuine and pressing injustice, more Canadians are ready to break the rules to, as they see it, set things right. One in five Canadians thinks it's acceptable to steal in order to feed your family, and this is a position whose acceptance increases among younger people.

Okay to Steal to Feed Family			
All Canadians	Elders	Boomers	Gen Xers
18%	12%	16%	24%

The Elders, many of whom have been through economic hardship, feel that there are always alternatives to theft. In many cases they made it the hard way—by working, often in thankless jobs—and they think this is far preferable to stealing. Many young people would disagree. They see extreme economic inequality (the kind that forces some into destitution) as injustice, plain and simple—and no loyalty to government, to businesses or to the infamous "system" would discourage them from taking responsive action.

In 1996, for the first time, families in Canada's bottom quintile (the lowest fifth of income earners) found their incomes down $2,000 from the previous year (from $15,000 to $13,000), while those in the top quintile increased their incomes by the same amount (from $136,000 to $138,000). No one really knows what impact the decrease had on the lives of Canada's poor. Did it motivate them to get off welfare and get a decent job, as the neo-conservatives argued it would?

The day after these statistics appeared in the newspaper, a wealthy couple living in Toronto's posh Forest Hill neighbourhood were carjacked and held for ransom by members of the city's underclass. It seems that if the Canadian state refuses to play Robin Hood, some of the poor will take the initiative and engage in do-it-yourself income redistribution.

Violent crime may be declining in Canada, but property crime is not. And for many Canadians, there is a self-righteousness about this theft. Those who steal property see themselves as postmodern socialist heroes of a sort, taking from the rich and giving to the less rich—themselves. Today, the anarchist philosopher Pierre Proudhon's assertion that "property is theft" probably has as many adherents in Canada as in the former Soviet Union.

In accepting the Academy Award in 1999 for his movie *Life Is Beautiful,* the Italian filmmaker Roberto Benigni thanked his parents for giving him "the greatest gift in life, the gift of poverty." Few children on this globe would thank their parents for such a gift because most know (or at least have a strong sense) that the largest number of those born into poverty can expect only an incremental improvement over their parents' circumstances during their lives.

When I was growing up, I came into contact with people who envisioned a Canada in which greater economic and social mobility was possible. Of course, all these dreaming Boomers were middle class. Everyone I knew in Walkerton in the 1950s was middle class. Everyone I knew in Rexdale in the 1960s was middle class. At university we were all middle class, except those who were upper middle class (I was meeting these people for the first time), the sons and daughters of Canada's doctors, lawyers and senior bureaucrats in business and government. If the world was not fair, my bourgeois peers and I imagined, we would make it so through acts of public policy. If we didn't agree with Pierre Trudeau that Canada was a just society, we certainly did agree that there were plenty of things we could do to rectify the situation. Some of my friends were Liberals, New Democrats and Red

Tories; others were even more radically idealistic, believing in revolutionary social change and seeing themselves in its vanguard.

As it turned out, the world moved to the right, not the left, and idealism gave way to self-interest. The energy that once might have gone into making the world a better place is now going into making each individual's personal life less threatening and more interesting. Institutions are more likely to be seen as impediments to self-actualization than as facilitators of it. We have replaced our faith in institutions and traditional Judeo-Christian moral values with faith in ourselves and in Adam Smith's invisible hand of market capitalism. And so we as a nation have arrived at a place in which some of us are willing to cheat our employers, our governments, others' businesses and sometimes even each other. But have Canadians become morally bankrupt? I think not. I would argue that we are in the midst of a transition. We have abandoned our traditional values—values that were imposed on us, and that we adopted out of a deep fear of reprisal, embarrassment or even damnation—and are just starting to seek out new moral norms. Ultimately, I believe we will enter a postmodern world in which individualism and personal autonomy will be tempered by deeply felt social bonds. In this world we will acknowledge our interdependence, honour communities of choice, respect the administrative mechanisms through which we maintain them and be more charitable towards friends and strangers, appreciating their role in the social fabric that surrounds us. In the meantime, many of us are, like children or adolescents testing the moral boundaries of their families and peer groups, just trying to see what we can get away with.

One thing we try to get away with is tax evasion. Canadians pay out nearly half their incomes in one sort of tax or another, nearly one-third more than Americans. Given the remarkably high levels of taxation in this country, it is amazing not how *much* resentment there is towards our tax scheme, but rather how *little* there is. Most of us still believe that in spite of our working for the government until noon every Wednesday, life is better here than in the U.S.

Nonetheless, a significant segment of the population is, to say the least, displeased with the compulsory redistribution of wealth. About one-sixth of Canadians feel it's okay to cheat on your taxes, as long as you don't get caught. Those most likely to say this are the Anxious Communitarians, one-quarter of whom feel this way. Those least likely to agree are the Cosmopolitan Modernists, only 4 per cent of whom think that tax evasion is acceptable. As I have noted elsewhere, Cosmopolitan Modernists have great respect for the principles associated with living in Canadian society. They may be unwilling to defer to arbitrary rules or authority, but they are not willing to throw out old values simply because they're old. CosMods are inclined to think critically about their adherence to rules, and in their opinion the rule that says "Pay your taxes; this society is worth it" makes sense. The Anxious Communitarians are somewhat more difficult to decode here. Why would a tribe that is so nationalistic be so averse to paying taxes, relative to the other tribes in the cohort? The answer resides in their sense of fatalism, and their belief that they have very little control over their own destinies. This tribe is resigned to the fact that there will always be poverty, and that they will not be able to change this even if they are motivated to that end. Luckily for them, most of the members of this tribe have ended up on the upper half of the wheel of fortune (although it will be interesting to check in with these rapacious consumers around retirement). They've got theirs, so to speak, and if the government's attempts to redistribute funds isn't going to solve the problem of poverty in any real or lasting way, they may as well duck out of the system to whatever extent they can.

Many of the Canadians who consider tax evasion to be acceptable behaviour feel as they do because they resent the uses to which their money is put by the government, as well as the "bleeding heart" ideology behind the redistribution of wealth in general. A parable circulating on the Internet conveys this resentment:

The Ant and the Grasshopper—Classic Version

The ant works hard in the withering heat all summer long, building his house and laying in supplies for the winter. The grasshopper thinks he's a fool, and laughs and dances and plays the summer away.

Come winter, the ant is warm and well fed. The grasshopper has no food or shelter, so he dies out in the cold.

Modern Canadian Version

The ant works hard in the withering heat all summer long, building his house and laying in supplies for the winter. The grasshopper thinks he's a fool, and laughs and dances and plays the summer away.

Come winter, the shivering grasshopper calls a press conference and demands to know why the ant should be allowed to be warm and well fed while others are cold and starving. The CBC shows up to provide pictures of the shivering grasshopper next to video of the ant in his comfortable home with its table filled with food.

Canada is stunned by the sharp contrast. How can it be that in a country of such wealth, this poor grasshopper is allowed to suffer so?

Then a representative of the NAGB (National Association of Green Bugs) shows up on CTV and charges the ant with "green bias," making the case that the grasshopper is the victim of 30 million years of anti-greenism. Kermit the Frog appears on TV with the grasshopper, and everybody cries when he sings "It's Not Easy Being Green."

Aline and Jean Chrétien make a special guest appearance on the CBC *National* news to tell a concerned Peter Mansbridge that they will do everything they can for the grasshopper, who has been denied the prosperity he deserves by those who benefited unfairly during the Mulroney summers, or as Chrétien refers to it, "the temperatures of the 1980s."

An NDP MP claims, in an interview with Mike Duffy, that the ant has got rich on the back of the grasshopper, and he calls for an immediate tax hike for the ant to make him pay his "fair share."

Finally, Parliament drafts the Economic Equity and Anti-Greenism Act and makes it retroactive to the beginning of the summer. The ant is fined for failing to hire a proportionate number of green bugs and, because he has nothing left to pay his retroactive taxes, his home is confiscated by the government.

Chrétien gets his old law firm to represent the grasshopper in the defamation suit against the ant, and the case is tried before a panel of federal judges. The ant loses the case.

As the story ends, we see the grasshopper finishing up the last bits of the ant's food while the government house he's in, which just happens to be the ant's old house, crumbles around him because he doesn't maintain it.

The ant has disappeared in the snow. And on the TV, which the grasshopper bought by selling most of the ant's food, they are showing Jean Chrétien standing before a wildly applauding group of Liberals and announcing that a new era of "fairness" has dawned in Canada.

The palpable anger in this little story says a lot about the way some Canadians feel towards the system that many are so proud of. Would those who penned this piece (or those who sent it to their friends and colleagues) be willing to cheat on their taxes to avoid paying into a system they see as so obviously out of control? Likely some would. Most have taken the more conventional action of supporting Mike Harris's Ontario Conservatives or the new Canadian Alliance. And of course many who cheat on their taxes do so not for ideological reasons (i.e., a belief that the government spends their money foolishly, or that the redistribution of wealth is in all cases unjustifiable) but out of simple selfishness.

Whether we are cheating the government, a private business or even another person, our behaviours of course reflect the way we feel towards institutions and our fellow citizens.

Although many of us may imagine that "thieves" are criminals on the fringes of society, mere blips on the cultural screen, this chapter has illustrated that the proportion of Canadians who would be willing to steal from organizations or individuals if given a convenient opportunity is substantial. Because the thieves among us are not a handful of alien rogues but a large number of our relatives, friends, co-workers and acquaintances, it is important that we consider the sociocultural currents that lead to fraudulent behaviour. I would posit that the surprising replies to the questions our survey posed are symptoms of our national liminal status with respect to everyday ethics.

No longer can religious institutions or bureaucratic organizations cause us to fall neatly into line by virtue of their authoritative might. And although many of us are beginning to replace internalized guilt with a strong sense of social responsibility in this new heterarchical world, we are still cutting our moral teeth. If threats of punishment, social stigmatization and damnation now seem hollow, is there any reason why we should be honest with government, business or each other? After years of learning ethics by rote, many Canadians are only now beginning to develop their own personal answers to this basic moral question.

9.

Money and Happiness

Again I tell you, it is easier for a camel to go through the eye of a needle than for a rich man to enter the kingdom of God.
—Matthew 19:24

Those who say that money can't buy happiness don't know where to shop.
—Anonymous

After all is said and done—when our spending has
been scrutinized, the value of our time and labour quantified,
our fear of the future translated into RRSP contributions and
our guilt and altruism transformed miraculously into charitable donations—the one question still whispering to us from
the backs of our minds is, of course, an old one: Does money
actually make us happy? I thought it appropriate to end this
book with a consideration of the impact our financial circumstances have on our psychological and emotional well-being.
After all, in the preceding chapters I have argued that our
social values—in other words, the way we see the world—fundamentally inform our financial behaviour. But that relationship is a two-way street; to some extent, at least, our finances
affect the way we see the world.

If we feel we've been dealt an unfair hand by life (or by
the economy or "the system"), we may be less likely, like the
Disengaged Darwinists, to be sympathetic to the pleas of
others for assistance: "Nobody's ever given *me* a free lunch;
why should my taxes allow anyone else to sit around all
day?" Conversely, we may feel, like the Cosmopolitan
Modernists, that we have enjoyed advantages that others
have not experienced, and that we therefore have a certain
duty to level the playing field with contributions to charitable
organizations or votes for political parties that are proponents of generously funded social programs. Risk-aversion,
generosity, attention to legacy, attitudes towards employment—in myriad ways, the extent to which we have or have
not enjoyed financial security affects the way we understand
society and our place in it. In addition, money also affects our
feelings about our own lives—that is, what psychologists
have termed our "subjective well-being" (SWB), or in lay
terms, our happiness.

Are people with more money happier than those with less? The answer is a heavily qualified yes. Numerous studies, including our own, have found that happiness and affluence are linked in some way, but the correlation is certainly not direct. In a 1995 article entitled "Who Is Happy?" the psychologists David G. Myers and Ed Deiner noted that "once people are able to afford life's necessities, increasing levels of affluence matter surprisingly little." In other words, happiness increases with wealth up to a certain point—the point at which basic human needs are met—but any affluence beyond that basic level is no guarantee of added happiness.

> The two top indexed values for happy people are need for autonomy and adaptability to complexity. The top indexed values for unhappy people are aimlessness and anomie. In general, those who are happy harbour modern values, with some notable exceptions (e.g., religiosity), while those who are unhappy harbour traditional values, especially the status-seeking values of importance of physical beauty and ostentatious consumption.

Environics research is largely consistent with this observation, but we have noted an additional trend. As people move out of the lowest income brackets into what is commonly understood as the middle class, there is some increase in the proportion of respondents who report that they are happy. Thereafter, the proportion of respondents who report that they are happy, as Myers and Deiner note in their own work, does not increase substantially until household income begins to exceed about $80,000 annually. As respondents move into the upper middle class, we see another increase in the proportion who report that they are happy more often than they are unhappy, as the bar chart on the next page illustrates.

The reason for this pattern seems to be that people in the middle class are not assailed by the same severe financial worries as those who are less affluent. Canadians who earn less than, say, $20,000 a year spend a greater proportion of

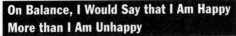

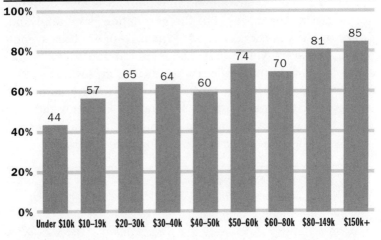

their income on basic necessities such as food, clothing and shelter. Thus they have less disposable income not only to consume goods and services that might make life easier or more pleasant, but also to save for retirement or for purposes of general financial security. Constant worry about money, as many Canadians know, can significantly diminish the chances that one will be "happy" on a day-to-day basis.

When it comes to happiness, however, there is not a great deal of variation between those at the lower end of the middle class (i.e., those earning between $20,000 and $30,000 annually) and those at the upper end (i.e., those earning between $70,000 and $80,000 annually). There is a difference of only 5 per cent among those who report they are happy in those two groups. Members of the middle class enjoy greater financial security than their counterparts in the lower class and are not plagued by the same financial worries, but they do not have sufficient disposable income to consume some of the luxuries that would give them that extra hit of comfort they desire. These Canadians are reasonably secure—they're providing for themselves, putting some money away and indulging themselves occasionally—but they've got their eye on something more.

> *We thought we could buy happiness through technology, which seemed to promise increased efficiency and, of course (we now say with a sardonic grin), more leisure time. Though we still harbour positive feelings about technology in general, in recent years our enthusiasm has been tempered by anxieties. We are no longer as excited by new technologies as we were in the past, when we saw them as untarnished opportunities. Now we are more aware of their negative potential (e.g., job losses, unforeseen health and environmental consequences, invasions of our privacy). We see the dangers of using cellphones while driving, and we're annoyed by other people's indiscriminate use of mobile communications devices in airplanes, restaurants, theatres and other public places. We are irritated by the uninvited invasion of spam (e-mail advertising), which seems somehow more intrusive and personal than regular junk mail. Biotechnology has given us an abundance of genetically modified foods, and we fear that the multinationals' assurances of their safety are about as reliable as those of the nuclear engineers a generation ago who said a meltdown was virtually impossible. The acclaimed sci-fi hit of 1999, The Matrix, exploited yet again our anxiety that the tools we create will end up controlling us, rather than the other way around. At one time, technological advances were seen as a way to make everyone more equal. However, many Canadians believe that these advances mostly serve an elite and often threaten those they do not benefit. They believe the scenario depicted in the movie Blade Runner is coming true.*

As we move into the group of Canadians whose annual household incomes exceed $80,000 we find a marked jump in the number of respondents who report that they are happy. These Canadians are able not only to provide for themselves and put money away in anticipation of their retirement, but also to consume the hedonistic indulgences that can make life more pleasant. Although consumption in itself doesn't make us happy, many of us know what a welcome respite a vacation can be or how much pleasure a longed-for "toy" can bring. These things aren't essential to one's well-being, but they can certainly brighten one's week. Perhaps most important, affluence affords us more opportunities to exercise personal choice; autonomy and personal control are key ingredients in the lives of happy individuals. Myers and Deiner note that people living in collectivist cultures generally report lower levels of happiness than those living in individualistic cultures, "where norms more strongly support experiencing and expressing positive emotions." This finding is consistent with the observation that as our values become more modern and approach the bottom of the socio-cultural map (where individualism is of prime importance), we report being happier in general.

> *For the very well off, affluence buys much more than more toys and better experiences; it buys independence, enough money to tell anyone to F___ O__!, in the crudest sense.*
>
> *But then, plenty of Autonomous Rebels haven't needed financial security to say the same thing many times to people throughout their lives.*

How do Canadians understand their own financial circumstances? Are they hopeful or fearful about the future? Do they think they're better or worse off than their parents at the same age? Are they satisfied with their finances?

Young people are, on the whole, fairly optimistic about their personal financial futures, but they are considerably less sanguine about their *present* financial circumstances. Gen Xers are the respondents least likely to report that their financial situation is better than their parents' was when they were the same age.

Of all the tribes, the Cosmopolitan Modernists are the most likely to report that their financial situation is better than their parents'; the New Aquarians are the least likely. In many

Financial Situation Better than Parents' at Same Age			
All Canadians	*Elders*	*Boomers*	*Gen Xers*
55%	70%	53%	46%

cases, New Aquarians have been raised in comfortable, even affluent homes, but they have rejected mainstream consumer culture as well as the rat race. Having embraced voluntary simplicity, they are likely to be less well off financially than their parents, in part because they have deliberately made money less of a priority. This tribe is also the most likely of all to say that people who let work take over their lives are crazy. It's not just the young idealists who hold this position, though; more than three-quarters of all Canadians agree with that statement.

As for the financial destiny of the next generation, Canadians are fairly evenly divided. About one-third of us believe that the next generation will be better off than the current generation when its members have reached the same age, about one-third think it will be worse off and one-third think it will be in about the same position.

But perhaps the more important consideration is whether we're satisfied with our current lot. Only about one in ten Canadians report that they are very satisfied with their current financial situation. However, a further five in ten say that they are somewhat satisfied with their finances. Among the Boomers, the more traditional tribes (the Anxious Communitarians and the Disengaged Darwinists) are more satisfied, while the more modern tribes (the Connected Enthusiasts and the Autonomous Rebels) are less satisfied. In fact, Connected Enthusiasts are the least likely of all thirteen tribes to report being satisfied with their finances. As was noted in chapter 6, a lifetime of indulgence is catching up with these experience-loving Canadians, and the future is beginning to look less than rosy. Among the Gen Xers, the Security-seeking Ascetics are the most satisfied with their finances. These young Canadians are saving with all their

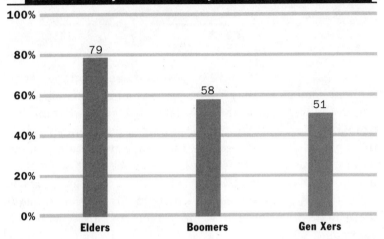

might, and when they look at the future they sigh happily (and a little smugly).

Though money offers us a feeling of security or apprehension when we consider the future, this is not the only way it can afford or deny us happiness. Most of us derive joy from parting with our money—that is, in consumption—but some of us are trying to cut back.

Among the Elders, there is a strong sense (73 per cent) that money is becoming less important for them personally.

In My Life, Money and Consumption Play a Less Important Role than Before			
All Canadians	Elders	Boomers	Gen Xers
52%	73%	52%	45%

Older Canadians, many of whom have already left the workforce and have bought most of what they plan to buy, feel strongly that money and consumption are less important than before. The Boomers, still front and centre in the rat race, are considerably less likely to agree with that sentiment.

Among the Boomers, the Autonomous Rebels are the most likely (56 per cent) to report that money and consumption are becoming less important in their lives, while the Disengaged Darwinists are the Boomer tribe least likely to agree.

Not surprisingly, it is the anti-consumerist New Aquarians of Generation X who are the most likely to report that money and consumption are becoming less significant in their lives; the consumption-happy Social Hedonists are the least likely to agree.

These tribal patterns repeat themselves in other consumption-related questions. For example, when faced with the statement "To buy myself something new is for me one of the greatest pleasures in life," the CosMods are least likely to agree (71 per cent either somewhat disagree or strongly disagree), followed by the Autonomous Rebels (30 per cent) and the New Aquarians (39 per cent) in their respective age groups. Predictably, the Extroverted Traditionalists among the Elders (64 per cent), the Anxious Communitarians among the Boomers (61 per cent) and the Thrill-seeking Materialists of Gen X (a whopping 80 per cent) are the most likely to say buying themselves something new is one of life's greatest pleasures.

When asked whether consumption plays a significant role in giving meaning and direction to their lives, only 1 per cent of Cosmopolitan Modernists say it is very important, while almost a quarter of Extroverted Traditionalists admitted that it gives them meaning. Only 1 per cent of Autonomous Rebels in the Boomer cohort agree, while Anxious Communitarians are the Boomer tribe most likely to agree. Among the youth tribes, the New Aquarians are the least likely to agree, but almost three in ten of their age peers in the Thrill-seeking Materialist tribe agree.

One final item is instructive as we examine the significance the various tribes ascribe to material success. When asked whether finances play a significant role in giving meaning and direction to their lives, Cosmopolitan Modernists are the least likely to agree; only 14 per cent of CosMods think this statement applies to them, compared with 34 per cent of Rational Traditionalists and a remarkable 53 per cent

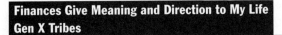

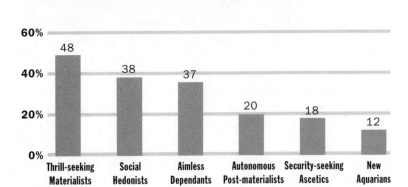

of Extroverted Traditionalists. In the Boomer tribe, only about one in ten Autonomous Rebels admits that finances are significant in giving them a sense of meaning, while almost half (49 per cent) of Anxious Communitarians do. Among Gen Xers, the New Aquarians are the least likely to feel that their finances give meaning to their lives, and Thrill-seeking Materialists are the most likely.

How does the significance that people ascribe to their consumption behaviours and finances relate to their happiness? The pattern is surprisingly consistent across the generations. Among the Elders, the Cosmopolitan Modernists who are strongest on deconsumption and are the least likely to see their finances as a defining aspect of their existence, are also the happiest tribe. Seventy-five per cent of Cosmopolitan Modernists report that they are happy more often than they are unhappy, while 71 per cent of Extroverted Traditionalists say the same. The Rational Traditionalists are the least happy tribe in the Elder cohort; only 63 per cent of these most traditional of Canadians report that they are happy most of the time.

In the Boomer cohort, the relationship between happiness and the significance ascribed to finances and consumption is even more clear-cut: the Autonomous Rebels, strongest on deconsumption, are the happiest tribe not only in their own cohort but of all thirteen tribes; fully 77 per cent of the Boomer Rebels report that they are happy. At the other end of the spectrum, the Anxious Communitarians, weakest on deconsumption and ascribing the most significance to their finances, are the least likely of the Boomer tribes to report that they are happy.

And, among the Gen Xers, it is the anti-materialist New Aquarians who most often (70 per cent) report being happy. However, there is little variation among the youth tribes, with only the Aimless Dependants reporting a significantly lower level of happiness than their age peers.

Autonomous Rebels are the happiest tribe, because they, more than any segment of Canadians to date, have achieved the ideal of autonomy. They are the defining tribe of their generation, which in turn is the defining generation of our present culture. They now dictate the agenda as citizens, as consumers, as workers. They gave us idealism in the 1960s, self-fulfillment in the 1970s, hedonism in the 1980s and (fiscal) responsibility in the 1990s. They are the tribe in their generation that has won life's lottery. And while they may have bitten off more idealism and personal gratification than they can chew, they know the stress of constant choices is infinitely preferable to a life of quiet resignation to or anger with a system that never allowed them to be themselves.

Why is Generation X, once stereotyped as collectively sulky and without purpose, so happy? And why do the Aimless Dependants stand out among their age peers? In answer to the first question, I would posit that the members of Generation X are enjoying the process of carving out their own lives and identities. As we have noted, Generation X is the most diverse generation of Canadians. As Canadians increasingly embrace diversity—not only ethnic and linguistic diversity, but also diversity of opinion and lifestyle—more and more young people are able to explore their own interests and ideals, to live their lives in ways that make sense to them without being

constrained by convention or stifling social mores. This freedom is breeding happiness among our young people because
they have experienced little else; while even the most open-
minded Boomers still recall the strictures of the traditional
homes and communities where they grew up, Gen Xers have
come of age in the society (created by their Boomer parents)
that was in part a reaction against the fetters of tradition and
conformity. Regardless of how they're choosing to live, or how
much money they're doing it on, Gen Xers are revelling in the
luxury of choice.

As for the second question, why Aimless Dependants
aren't enjoying the fluid society of the new millennium, the
answer is simple: the freedom that delights most Gen Xers
frightens the Aimless Dependants, who are change-averse
and intimidated by complexity. Aimless Dependants are
unhappy because the main thing they're comforted by—
structure—is disappearing. While the other tribes are happy
to engineer their own personal lives using their own priorities
(be they materialistic, social or political), the Aimless
Dependants are interested not in the content of a system
but in the system itself. They'd like someone to tell them
what's important—what success is, what the rules are, what
their role is supposed to be. While the other tribes derive happiness from filling in these answers for themselves, the
Aimless Dependants are disturbed by excessive amounts
of choice and freedom. More than anything, Aimless
Dependants fear the wide open sea described by Nietzsche in
The Gay Science:

> We have left the land and taken to our ship! We have
> burned our bridges—more, we have burned our land
> behind us! Now, little ship, take care! The ocean lies all
> around you; true, it is not always roaring, and some-
> times it lies there as if it were silken and golden and a
> gentle favourable dream. But there will be times when
> you will know that it is infinite and that there is nothing
> more terrible than infinity. . . . Alas, if homesickness for

land should assail you, as if there were more *freedom* there—and there is no longer any "land"!

Unfortunately for the Aimless Dependants, but fortunately for more adaptable and self-directed Canadians, we as a society are moving further and further away from the "land" of codes and conventions, to which our forebears clung so resolutely, towards a space of greater freedom; we're navigating through chaos and complexity and, for those not afraid to pursue it in their own way, moving towards greater happiness.

In the end, though, I would posit that life in Canada isn't really about happiness, or at least not in the giddy, euphoric sense we often imagine. While the American Dream seems to have something to do with achieving a feeling of importance and good fortune, I believe that Canadians aspire to a quieter, humbler brand of subjective well-being: simple contentment. Life in Canada is increasingly about harmony, balance, self-esteem and tolerance for diversity. More and more, Canada is about values rather than rules, individuals rather than institutions, spontaneity rather than rituals, and an evolution from the thirst for achievement and material grandeur to a personal quest for spiritual meaning and individual growth. These trends do now, and will continue to, manifest themselves in our financial behaviour.

10.
Conclusion

During the preceding pages, I hope it has become clear to you that it is not only my personal bias as a social researcher that causes me to believe that Canadians' financial behaviours are strongly informed by their social values. I believe there is ample evidence to support the idea that money's growing importance in our culture does not signal the death of values outside the financial sphere but rather that money, by insinuating itself so deeply into our daily lives, has become a tool with which we can express ourselves and attempt to change our lives and our environments in the way we desire.

I have argued here, as I did in *Sex in the Snow*, that social change in Canada during the past few decades has been profound. Deference to patriarchal and institutional authority has plummeted, and our willingness to start (and in some cases end) our lives at the bottom of a hierarchy that someone else dreamed up has diminished substantially. Father doesn't know best any more (if he ever did) and Canadians are looking to make their own decisions about the things they value and the way they live. This particular brand of social change is part and parcel of our national journey along the trajectory from tradition through modernism towards the utopian postmodernism of the future. In these three paradigms, our social understanding of currency has been evolving along with our values. Under the traditional model, power was the currency of choice; in modernity, money became the central currency; currently we are becoming a postmodern people and seeing vitality—the ability to experience lives of energy and intensity—as the most desirable end in our society.

Our evolving social values, in addition to changing our ideas about currency itself, are affecting our behaviours in a number of practical financial arenas. In the workplace, we desire greater autonomy and personal freedom. We are less willing to accept the edicts of tyrannical employers, and we are demanding more control over the work we do and the way we do it. Many of us are turning to self-employment as a means of achieving the autonomy we desire, and those who are still working for someone else are trying to do so on their own terms.

In the world of consumption, the other-directed values of modernity are melting away: our purchases are becoming less conspicuous. We want the shopping experience to be quick and convenient when we're in a rush, or more experiential and sensuously rich when we're looking to indulge ourselves. More of us are putting our money where our consciences are as we try to do business with humane and ethical organizations. Certainly, some of us are still out to impress the neighbours, but the trend of the future is towards making personally meaningful purchases rather than flashy ones.

Those of us who are saving our money (and some of us aren't—yet) are doing so in ways we can control and monitor ourselves. Traditional savings accounts and authoritative financial gurus are making less and less sense for modern Canadians. We're beginning to seek out new advisers, often on a casual basis, discussing investment decisions with friends and colleagues, and we're trusting ourselves to take care of our own financial affairs. Using the Internet to gather information and participate directly in the stock market, we're hoping to develop portfolios and long-term financial plans that are both personalized and profitable.

Charitable giving too is registering our desire for greater personal control. Trends like donor-directed giving are signalling an unwillingness on the part of Canadian philanthropists to throw money at causes they don't understand or that don't seem to be effecting real change. Our donations, like our purchases and in some cases our jobs, reflect our social values; this is evidenced by the fact that younger Canadians are choosing new secular destinations for their charitable gifts rather than sending cheques to the churches and synagogues their parents and grandparents have long supported.

With respect to financial ethics, we are in a liminal period. No longer willing to defer automatically to traditional moralizing or threats of punishment in the afterlife, some Canadians are asking themselves whether there's any point in enacting the ethics they were taught as children. The upstanding moral behaviour of the early adopters in Generation X, however, indicates that as Canadians find their own personal moral codes and reason out their own systems of ethics, our society may just become more honest—and more genuinely so—than it has ever been.

Is our money making us happy? Depending on the amount we have and the importance we ascribe to it, yes. In general, those with more money tend to report higher levels of happiness than those with less money. That said, there is strong evidence to support the idea that it is not money itself or the things money can buy that we value, but rather the freedom money affords us. Sure, some Canadians like the Extroverted Traditionalists who have grown up believing that material comfort and security are the ultimate goals in life have learned to value money above almost all else. But the fact that the members of Generation X, regardless of their financial situations or attitudes towards money, are (with the exception of the Aimless Dependants) all remarkably happy would seem to indicate that it is the personal autonomy, which is becoming more prevalent in our society, that is the *real* treasure. Young Canadians are going their own ways—some, yes, in pursuit of the almighty dollar, others in pursuit of social justice, and still others are just looking for the next party. It is the freedom to make these personal journeys that seems to be putting a smile on the face of Canada's youth.

In my altogether ironic subtitle, I said this book would be about Canadians, money and the meaning of life. Most readers would agree that Canadians and money have been adequately covered, but some may wonder whether I've offered the promised conclusion regarding the meaning of life. It is only in our examination of the subjective well-being we normally call happiness that the final theme comes more clearly into focus. In the last chapter, we saw that money does and does not buy happiness. We see that it is possible to have too little but not too much, although there are happy people who have very little and wealthy people who are miserable.

Above all, it is our analysis of the tribes that offers the greatest insight into the meaning of life for Canadians. Just as we are seeing an increase in the number of social values tribes in our culture, so too are we seeing an increase in the number of ways in which people find meaning in their lives and achieve happiness. We see one tribe that achieves happiness, after having survived war and economic depression, by living according to the traditional norms of religion, the family and materialism: the Extroverted Traditionalists of the Elder cohort. We see another, the Autonomous Rebels, the defining tribe of the Boomer cohort, that has achieved happiness by rejecting traditional values and embracing autonomy, equality and personal fulfillment. Among the youth, almost all the tribes at this early stage in their lives are finding meaning and happiness: the materialistic Thrill-seekers, the expressive Social Hedonists, the conservative Security-seeking Ascetics, the idealistic New Aquarians and the ultra-individualistic Autonomous Post-materialists. Only the lonely souls among the Aimless Dependant youth tribe seem to be out of sync with the mega-currents in our culture. These lost warriors cannot find meaning and happiness in a culture that no longer values powerful institutions, patriarchal authority and the certainty that comes from demographic stereotypes. Their only escape from the pluralism, relativism and contingency of our era is the violence celebrated in popular culture and occasionally in their own lives.

I suppose it makes sense that those who feel best about themselves and their lives are those whose lives are most congruent with the values held in highest esteem by our society. In other cultures at other times, the happiest people have been the warriors, the priests, the artists, the merchants. In our world, values are displacing demographics as determinants of our life choices and life chances. Autonomy and diversity will define Canada in the twenty-first century and the tribes that see opportunities and not threats in these mega-currents will be the winners.

So we see that in order to truly understand our society—both in practical terms and in ideological terms—it is essential that we understand both our ideas *and* our finances. These two facets of Canadian life and the Canadian identity are inextricably bound up in each other, and a true knowledge of either necessitates a deep sensitivity to both. An examination of Canada's social values tribes and their attitudes about money yields what I believe to be a fascinating portrait of our nation, and one that will become increasingly nuanced as more and more Canadians exercise their right to live in the ways they find most fulfilling, and as new Canadians—those not yet born and those now living in other parts of the world—introduce their own values into our evolving culture.

Appendix A

Canada's Thirteen Social Values Tribes

The Elders

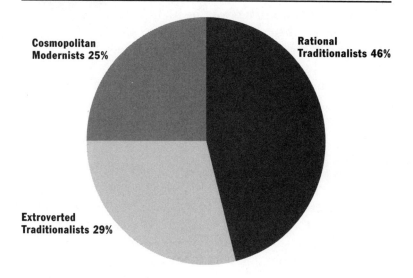

Cosmopolitan Modernists 25%

Rational Traditionalists 46%

Extroverted Traditionalists 29%

Rational Traditionalists

Key Demographics
Population
Proportion of Canadian population: 12 per cent
Proportion of Elders: 46 per cent
Total number in Canada: 3,658,600

Other Demographics
Higher-than-average proportion in communities of fewer
    than 5,000 people
Fundamental Motivation
Financial Independence, Security and Stability
Key Values
Risk-aversion
Rationality
Respect for Historical Tradition
Respect for Authority
Duty
Deferred Gratification
Words to Live By
"Follow your head, not your heart."
"Better safe than sorry."
"A bird in the hand is worth two in the bush."
Icons
Former British prime minister Winston Churchill
Television character Ward Cleaver
Former businessman and politician C. D. Howe
Former American president Franklin D. Roosevelt
Movie star John Wayne
Ontario premier Mike Harris
The Unknown Soldier
Money Orientation
Making it: "I'm looking forward to the gold watch of
    retirement after a lifetime of hard work."
Spending it: Price and pragmatism
Saving it: "A penny saved is a penny earned."
Giving it away: Church/synagogue/mosque
Stealing it: "I'm no deadbeat thief."

Extroverted Traditionalists

Key Demographics
Population
Proportion of Canadian population: 7 per cent

Proportion of Elders: 29 per cent
Total number in Canada: 2,134,400
Other Demographics
Higher-than-average proportion in Quebec
Higher-than-average proportion are women
Fundamental Motivation
Traditional Communities, Institutions and Social Status
Key Values
Religiosity
Family
Respect for Historical Tradition
Respect for Institutions
Duty
Fear
Deferred Gratification
Words to Live By
"Respect your elders."
"A penny saved is a penny earned."
"Spare the rod and spoil the child."
"Adam and Eve, not Adam and Steve."
"It's God's will."
Icons
Prime Minister Jean Chrétien
Former Quebec premier Maurice Duplessis
Jesus Christ
TV character June Cleaver
Mother Teresa
Money Orientation
Making it: "I've been a good husband/wife, mother/
    father, employee all my life; that's how people
    know me."
Spending it: "Wait till the neighbours see *this*."
Saving it: "Better safe than sorry (or so my adviser says)."
Giving it away: Church/synagogue/mosque
Stealing it: Thou shalt not.

Cosmopolitan Modernists

Key Demographics
Population
Proportion of Canadian population: 6 per cent
Proportion of Elders: 25 per cent
Total number in Canada: 1,829,500
Other Demographics
Mostly mirror the general population
Fundamental Motivation
Personal Autonomy and Experience-seeking
Key Values
Control of Destiny
Global World-view
Respect for Education
Desire for Innovation
Community Involvement
Words to Live By
"The world is my oyster."
"Take time to smell the roses."
"Think globally, act locally."
Icons
Author Pierre Berton
Citizen of the global village Maurice Strong
Columnist Dalton Camp
Author John Kenneth Galbraith
Former governor general Jeanne Sauvé
Money Orientation
Making it: Doing well, living well
Spending it: "Do I need it? Will it really make me happy?"
Saving it: "A little risk can go a long way."
Giving it away: Medical, educational and religious causes:
    body, mind, spirit
Stealing it: "If you don't like the system, don't cheat it—
    change it."

The Boomers

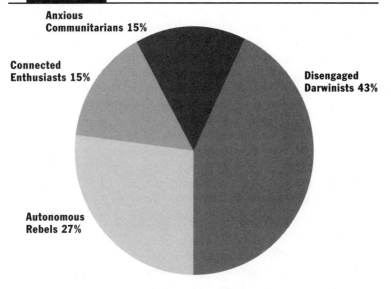

Anxious Communitarians 15%

Connected Enthusiasts 15%

Disengaged Darwinists 43%

Autonomous Rebels 27%

Autonomous Rebels

Key Demographics
Population
Proportion of Canadian population: 11 per cent
Proportion of Boomers: 27 per cent
Total number in Canada: 3,354,000
Other Demographics
Higher-than-average proportion in British Columbia
Higher-than-average incomes
Higher-than-average proportion have completed
    post-secondary education
Higher-than-average proportion are professionals
Fundamental Motivation
Personal Autonomy and Self-fulfillment
Key Values
Scepticism towards Traditional Institutions
Suspicion of Authority

Freedom
Individuality
Words to Live By
"Knowledge is power."
"I did it my way."
"The personal is political."
Icons
Governor General Adrienne Clarkson
Philosopher and critic Mark Kingwell
Talk-show host Pamela Wallin
Environmentalist David Suzuki
Hillary and Bill Clinton
Martin Luther King Jr.
Feminist Gloria Steinem
John Lennon
Money Orientation
Making it: "I want my work to mean something, but I
  don't want it to mean everything."
Spending it: No frills, just function. Will pay for quality
  and convenience.
Saving it: "Gotta risk some to make some; I know what
  I'm doing."
Giving it away: Medical and social causes
Stealing it: "Depends on the situation, but don't cheat the
  little guy."

Anxious Communitarians

Key Demographics
Population
Proportion of Canadian population: 6 per cent
Proportion of Boomers: 15 per cent
Total number in Canada: 1,829,400
Other Demographics
Higher-than-average proportion are white-collar workers
Fundamental Motivation
Traditional Communities, Institutions and Social Status

Key Values
Consumerism
Deference to Authority
Need for Respect
Words to Live By
"Dress for success."
"It's only common sense."
"Don't rock the boat."
"Buy it—it's on sale."
Icons
Household guru Martha Stewart
Talk-show host Oprah Winfrey
Comedian Tim Allen
TV personality Bill Cosby
Money Orientation
Making it: "My job is one of the ways I show myself and others who I am."
Spending it: "Show me the label."
Saving it: "I leave it to the experts. I don't want to do anything rash or foolish."
Giving it away: Religious organizations
Stealing it: "Might as well take what I can get while I can get it. If I don't someone else will."

Connected Enthusiasts

Key Demographics
Population
Proportion of Canadian population: 6 per cent
Proportion of Boomers: 15 per cent
Total number in Canada: 1,829,400
Other Demographics
Higher-than-average proportion are professionals
Higher-than-average proportion are white-collar workers *or* unemployed
Fundamental Motivation
Self-exploration and Experience-seeking

Key Values

Self-exploration

Community

Experimentation

Hedonism

Words to Live By

"Age is a state of mind."

"Live for today."

"Eat, drink and be merry, for tomorrow we die."

"Forever young."

"Work to live, don't live to work."

Icons

Pop star Madonna

Filmmaker Denys Arcand

Pop star Celine Dion

Actress Shirley MacLaine

Money Orientation

Making it: "I need money to live as I wish, but I'd never
let work keep me from some fun with my friends."

Spending it: "What's new?"

Saving it: "I need my money now; I can't risk it in the
short term."

Giving it away: Religious and medical organizations

Stealing it: "Stealing is generally wrong."

Disengaged Darwinists

Key Demographics

Population

Proportion of Canadian population: 17 per cent

Proportion of Boomers: 43 per cent

Total number in Canada: 5,183,500

Other Demographics

Higher-than-average proportion are men

Higher-than-average proportion in Ontario

Higher-than-average proportion are blue-collar workers
or professionals

Fundamental Motivation

Financial Independence, Security and Stability

Key Values

Self-interest

Social Darwinism

Rationality

Simplicity

Desire for Money

Words to Live By

"It's the law of the jungle."

"Every man for himself."

"Look out for Number One."

"Survival of the fittest."

"I read it in the *Post*/the *Sun*."

Icons

Ontario premier Mike Harris

Columnist Barbara Amiel

Sports commentator Don Cherry

TV character Al Bundy

Hockey player Eric Lindros

Money Orientation

Making it: "Show me the money."

Spending it: "They have everything I want at
     Canadian Tire; their stuff is cheap, and it works."

Saving it: Slow and steady

Giving it away: Religious organizations

Stealing it: "I was raised knowing right from wrong.
     Stealing is wrong."

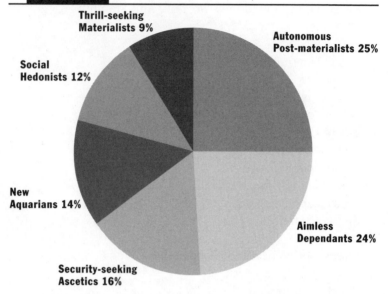

Aimless Dependants

Key Demographics
  Population
  Proportion of Canadian population: 8 per cent
  Proportion of Gen Xers: 24 per cent
  Total number in Canada: 2,439,300
  Other Demographics
  Higher-than-average proportion are blue-collar workers
    or unemployed
  Higher-than-average proportion in communities of fewer
    than 5,000 people
Fundamental Motivation
  Financial Independence, Security and Stability
Key Values
  Ostentatious Consumption
  Desire for Independence

Fatalism
Nihilism
Words to Live By
"What's the system ever done for me?"
"Get out of my face."
"F**k it, motherf*****!"
"It doesn't matter who you vote for—the government
always wins."
Icons
WWF star the Rock
Rap artist Eminem
Metal band Slipknot
Talk-show host Jerry Springer
Money Orientation
Making it: "My job is just a paycheque."
Spending it: "I don't care if kids in Indonesia made it.
How much is it?"
Saving it: "It's *my* money; I'd better not lose any."
Giving it away: "What has anyone ever done for *me*?"
Stealing it: *"Carpe diem."*

Thrill-seeking Materialists

Key Demographics
Population
Proportion of Canadian population: 3 per cent
Proportion of Gen Xers: 9 per cent
Total number in Canada: 914,700
Other Demographics
Mostly mirror the general population
Fundamental Motivation
Traditional Communities, Social Status and
Experience-seeking
Key Values
Desire for Money and Material Possessions
Desire for Recognition, Respect and Admiration
Aesthetics

555

Words to Live By
"Money is power."
"It's not how you play the game—it's whether you win."
"I feel the need for speed."

Icons
Former basketball superstar Michael Jordan
Current basketball star Vince Carter
Singer/actress Jennifer Lopez
Singer Shania Twain
Actress Pamela Lee Anderson
Rap star Jay-Z

Money Orientation
Making it: "I want two things out of a job: a cheque and a title."
Spending it: "I need chic and I need it now."
Saving it: "Already? What for?"
Giving it away: Medical charities, if at all
Stealing it: Too busy shopping

New Aquarians

Key Demographics
Population
Proportion of Canadian population: 5 per cent
Proportion of Gen Xers: 14 per cent
Total number in Canada: 1,524,600
Other Demographics
Mostly mirror the general population

Fundamental Motivation
Social Justice and Experience-seeking

Key Values
Adaptability
Concern for the Less Fortunate
Concern for the Environment
Respect for Education
Contempt for Traditional Authorities
Hedonism

Words to Live By

"There is no being, only becoming."

"Everything changed in Seattle."

"No justice, no peace."

Icons

Singer Sarah McLachlan

Author Naomi Klein

Singer/activist Jello Biafra

Rap-metal group Rage Against the Machine

Author/activist John Zerzan

Hip-hop group dead prez

Money Orientation

Making it: "I'd never do work I didn't believe in."

Spending it: "When I must consume at all, I consume with conscience."

Saving it: "I'm not saving much now, but when I do I'll call the shots."

Giving it away: Environmental and social causes

Stealing it: "No, thanks."

Autonomous Post-materialists

Key Demographics

Population

Proportion of Canadian population: 9 per cent

Proportion of Gen Xers: 25 per cent

Total number in Canada: 2,744,200

Other Demographics

Higher-than-average proportion are students

Higher-than-average proportion are single

Fundamental Motivation

Personal Autonomy and Self-fulfillment

Key Values

Freedom

Spontaneity

Words to Live By

"It's my life."

"Do your own thing."

"Image is nothing."

Icons

Dot-com millionaires (any of them)

Computer hacker Mafiaboy

Editor Richard Martineau

Bart Simpson

Apple co-founder Steve Jobs

Basketball star Dennis Rodman

Tennis players Venus and Serena Williams

Animated character Eric Cartman

Money Orientation

Making it: "Freedom and personal satisfaction are my priorities."

Spending it: "Experiences, not stuff."

Saving it: "I'm testing the market so I can make my own decisions when the time comes."

Giving it away: Medical charities

Stealing it: "From the market, but not from regular people."

Social Hedonists

Key Demographics

Population

Proportion of Canadian population: 4 per cent

Proportion of Gen Xers: 12 per cent

Total number in Canada: 1,219,700

Other Demographics

Higher-than-average proportion are teenagers

Fundamental Motivation

Hedonism and New Communities

Key Values

Risk-taking

Aesthetics

Sexual Permissiveness

Immediate Gratification

Words to Live By

"Don't worry, be happy."

"If you look good, you feel good."

"My friends are my family."

"Pass the joint."

Icons

Race-car driver Jacques Villeneuve

Extreme sports athletes

Pop-punk band Blink 182

Pop star Ricky Martin

Movie character Austin Powers

Rap star Sisqo

Money Orientation

Making it: "Show me the money."

Spending it: "If it's not the latest, it's not for me."

Saving it: "I'll start saving when fashion stands still."

Giving it away: "Why?"

Stealing it: "Why not?"

Security-seeking Ascetics

Key Demographics

Population

Proportion of Canadian population: 6 per cent

Proportion of Gen Xers: 16 per cent

Total number in Canada: 1,829,500

Other Demographics

Higher-than-average proportion are women

Higher-than-average proportion have young kids

Fundamental Motivation

Family, Security and Stability

Key Values

Security

Simplicity

Deferred Gratification

Words to Live By

"My kids are my life."

"Tried, tested and true."
"Home is where the heart is."
"Some values are timeless."
"Make hay while the sun shines."

Icons

Their own parents and grandparents
Russell Crowe in the film *Gladiator*
Any mother protecting her kids
Talk-show host Rosie O'Donnell
Finance Minister Paul Martin

Money Orientation

Making it: "I'd prefer a job that offered me satisfaction, but stability is my top priority."
Spending it: Trying not to
Saving it: Doggedly
Giving it away: Religious and medical charities
Stealing it: No way

Appendix B

Methodology: A Technical Description of the Theoretical Foundations of the 3SC Map

The underlying roots of the 3SC system for monitoring changes in social values go back more than a century and a half to a curious young Frenchman named Alexis de Tocqueville. De Tocqueville visited the United States in the 1830s to examine, first-hand, the social and political life of the world's "first new nation." His *Democracy in America* is to social values research what Adam Smith's *Wealth of Nations* is to economics. Later in the nineteenth century, the economist Thorstein Veblen took another giant step forward in the description and understanding of changes to human social values with his *Theory of the Leisure Class.*

In our century, social scientists such as Abraham Maslow, David Riesman, Daniel Bell, Milton Rokeach and Louis Leon Thurstone explored the impacts and dynamics of changing social values in contemporary society. They also identified a hierarchy of social values; for example, Maslow saw a structure of values that rose from those associated with basic physical survival up the ladder to those associated with self-actualization at the highest intellectual and moral levels.

The Scandinavian sociologist Stein Rokeach defined values as having the following properties:

■ they are beliefs;
■ they refer to a mode of conduct or established orientation towards existence; and
■ they are preferences, as well as conceptions, of personal and social ideals.

The 3SC methodology was developed in the 1960s by Alain de Vulpian and our French colleagues at Cofremca, whose clients wished to understand the evolution and meaning of the spontaneous rejection of traditional values and institutions evident among many young people in Western societies at that time. Their initial knowledge of social values came from extensive qualitative research, primarily in-depth, one-on-one interviews. This research revealed new attitudes towards order, religious and secular authority, success, social status, the role of the sexes and the place of youth in society, as well as a growing orientation of individuals towards personal autonomy, informality and immediate gratification.

In the early 1970s, the knowledge gained from the qualitative research was used to create questions and scales designed to measure the diffusion of the new values within French culture. This was accomplished through annual quantitative surveys of representative samples of the population. The resulting Système Cofremca de Suivi des Courants Socio-Culturels—or 3SC—was subsequently extended beyond France into more than twenty countries in Europe and the Americas; it came to Canada in 1983 and the United States in 1992.

Principal components analysis of the socio-cultural currents tracked in the annual surveys, followed by factor analysis of correspondence of those social value trends, has revealed three major axes, or dimensions, of social change in Western societies:

- conformity versus individuality;
- other- versus inner-directedness; and
- asceticism/moralism versus hedonism.

The axes of social change that emerge from the 3SC analysis in North America are congruent with those that social scientists have deduced in studying the evolution of modern culture on other continents as well. This framework is further enhanced by ongoing qualitative research studies that probe the evolution of values, mental postures and social meaning in particular cultures.

For example, the other-directed end of the spectrum tracks values that reflect such dimensions as emulation (status recognition), the need to belong (to family or community or country) and the need to assert oneself socially (achievement and conspicuous consumption).

Meanwhile, the inner-directed end of the spectrum monitors values that focus on freedom and control, the need to escape from authority and discipline and the quest for personal fulfillment and authenticity.

In addition, 3SC has actively explored a range of values, from those that are security-driven (need for financial security, aversion to complexity and strangers) to those that are societally driven (need for affiliation and love) to higher-order values of self-actualization and social purpose (the desire to protect and conserve the environment, the sense of being a global citizen, the desire to protect nature and the rights of others, and so on).

Each year, the 3SC team assesses values influencing culture and consumption. This means not only tracking previously identified values but also probing for emerging trends and new mental postures and motivations.

The Measurement of Values

To fully understand the 3SC system, one must spend some time learning how it is that we create operational measures of each value and then analyze them in multivariate space. Again, we draw on both the work of other social scientists and our own empirical research to understand how best to assess each value and to explore the meaning of these values in our culture.

Measurement of the values involves the following steps:
1. Each value is measured using approximately two to five Likert-type questions. (These questions require answers which fall on a numerical scale indicating the intensity of a feeling or the frequency of a thought or activity. Respondents might be asked, for example, whether they

strongly agree, agree, disagree or strongly disagree with a given statement.)

2. The raw data for each question are standardized on 0–4 scales.

3. Individuals are assigned a score on each value. Their responses to each of the questions found by principle components analysis are added up to measure that value. The questions are weighted in this summation, following the results of the principal components analysis.

4. Each individual's overall score on that value is converted to a 0–100 point scale.

5. This same procedure is repeated for all the values until each individual is assigned a score between 0 and 100 on each value.

Analyzing and Interpreting the Social Values Together

We use factor analysis of correspondence to explore the associations between individuals and their standing on social values trends. From this analysis emerges a "map space solution," a set of axes that more generally underlie the collection of changing values we have assessed. These axes allow us to interpret the values together on one common map, to explore their relative positions with other values and to track their movements through time.

Individuals are assigned a set of axis coordinates that we use to plot subgroup positions, positions that can be used for descriptive purposes or positioning analysis. Subgroups of any type can be defined, for example:

- supporters of a political party or position;
- early adopter of technology;
- heavy brand users;
- generational cohorts;
- high-income earners;
- "somewhat satisfied" customers; or
- particularly strong believers in the value of ethical consumerism.

Profiling Subgroups in Terms of Their Social Values

In order to understand, in depth, the complete values portrait presented by a particular subgroup, we begin by plotting the distributions of all individual scores for each value. When this process is complete, we determine the cut-off point for the top quartile of scores for that value (that is, the scale point beyond which those 25 per cent of the population who are strongest on that value score). Owing to distributional considerations, this cut-off usually defines approximately 25 per cent, rather than the top quartile precisely, but this is not a problem for the subsequent analysis.

For a specific subgroup (e.g., residents of a certain region or users of a certain brand), we first create their distribution of scores on each value. We then compare the distribution of this subgroup with the distribution of the population as a whole.

Specifically, we look at what percentage of the subgroup has scores that are higher than the cut-off point used to define the top quartile of the general population. For example, the cut-off score for the general population might be 62. Knowing that 25 per cent of Canadians will score between 62 and 100, and finding that 47 per cent of a specific subgroup has scores higher than 62, the 3SC methodology shows that that particular subgroup is stronger than average on this particular value.

Next, we create an index number quantifying how much stronger or weaker than the general population a specific subgroup is on each value. The index numbers for each trend are created by dividing the percentage of the subgroup scoring above the cut-off by the percentage of the general population scoring above the cut-off (usually 25 per cent), and then multiplying by 100. (In the example above, 47 is divided by 25 and the result multiplied by 100. Thus the subgroup scores 188, meaning that its members score above the cut-off 88 per cent more frequently than Canadians in general.) This procedure is repeated for each value.

Inferential statistical tests are employed to determine the difference between the subgroup proportion exceeding the cut-off and the general population proportion exceeding the cut-off. If there is no difference, the value is not plotted on the subgroup's value profile map. Colour codes, according to a thermometer gradient, are then applied to the value labels when printing the statistically reliable trends on the map. These codes reflect the size of the index scores:

- A score of less than 60 means that the subgroup is much weaker on the value than average; it is colour-coded blue.
- A score of 60 to 99 (or the index score closest to 100 that is still statistically reliably different from the general population) means that the subgroup is somewhat weaker on the value than average; it is colour-coded green.
- A score of 101 to 139 (or the index score closest to 100 that is still statistically reliably different from the general population) means that the subgroup is somewhat stronger on the value than average; it is colour-coded orange.
- A score of 140 or higher means that the subgroup is much stronger on the value than average; it is colour-coded red.

Short-term Social Change

Short-term 3SC maps measure changes in the strengths of values from one year to the next. The distributions of scores between two years are compared to determine if there are statistically significant differences. This is completed first for the total population, then for specific subgroups.

Values that have gained in strength—that is, progressed—are coded in orange. Values that have lost in strength—that is, regressed—are coded in green. Values that have neither gained nor lost in strength are excluded from the map.

Long-term Social Change

Values that have moved in one consistent direction for three years or more, either continuously increasing or continuously decreasing, are identified as important long-term trends in social values change. These trends are plotted on the map of long-term evolution.

Trends that are in constant progression are colour-coded red. Trends that had been in constant progression but are now stabilized are colour-coded orange. Trends that had been in constant regression but are now stabilized are colour-coded green. Trends that are in constant regression are colour-coded blue.

Mapping and Segmentation

Next, we use a statistical technique called factor analysis of correspondence to create a mapping of the social values trends we have identified and measured in our research. This mapping presents the trends in such a way that those that are similar or correlated are positioned close to each other on the map. Those that are dissimilar are generally plotted on opposite sides of the map, far away from each other. And those that are unrelated are generally at right angles to each other (if you were to draw a line from them back through the centre of the map). Because the map works in several dimensions, these relationships are a bit approximate when shown only in the two dimensions we've illustrated with our map in this book.

Every person who takes part in our 3SC project is plotted and assigned coordinates on many axes, or dimensions, that emerge from the factor analysis of correspondence procedure. These dimensions are found in such a way that they maximally discriminate among people in terms of how they vary in their social values, with the "average" Canadian sitting right at the centre of the map. If we were to analyze individuals from a different culture, there is no guarantee that the map we would come up with would look the same, or even display the same axes that underlie the social values of Canadians. In fact, even the U.S. map has different axes from those found on the Canadian map; in other words, the axes found on the U.S.

map would not be effective in differentiating the social values of Canadians.

The average position of groups of people can be shown on the map. So we can plot the positions of old people and young people, men and women, Albertans and Nova Scotians, professionals and unionists, Catholics and Protestants and so on. We can also see the "positioning" of people who vote Liberal versus Alliance, jog versus bird-watch, buy Toyotas versus Fords, drink Coke versus Pepsi, read *Saturday Night* versus *Chatelaine,* or run PCs versus Macs. And if we have grouped people into "segments," or in this case what we call social values tribes, we can plot their positions too. The values that are plotted near to the average positions of groups often characterize the mental postures of those groups very well.

But how do we initially establish how many tribes or segments exist, and which people are members of which tribes? To do this, we use statistical techniques such as cluster analysis, the goal of which is to find clusters of people who are most like each other in terms of their social values and outlooks. The final clustering creates groups of people who are similar, or homogeneous, within their tribes and reasonably different between tribes. For purposes of our two books, *Sex in the Snow* and *Better Happy Than Rich?,* we divided the population into the three age cohorts of Elders, Boomers and Gen Xers, and conducted such a clustering within each cohort. The variables we analyzed to create the tribes using clustering were people's standing on each of the three main axes that constitute the Canadian map.

Appendix C

Finding Your Tribe: How Do YOU Compare with Other Canadians on Social Values?

If we haven't yet surveyed you in one of our annual studies to diagnose your social values, here is your chance to find out where you would sit on our social values map and to which tribe you belong. Please visit our website at *www.Environics.net* and follow the links to the 3SC social values page. There you will find a short form of our full social values questionnaire. Just fill it out and submit it, and we will calculate a general position for you on the map. We will also give you some indication of which tribe you are most likely a member of. Not everybody is clearly a member of one and only one tribe, and given that we can't ask you our whole battery of several hundred questions, we will produce a result that indicates how likely it is that you are a member of each tribe within your age cohort. Have fun, and remember to answer honestly and directly to get the best estimate of your tribal affiliation!

Bibliography

Adams, Michael. *Sex in the Snow.* Toronto: Penguin, 1997.

Brearton, Steve. "Why We Buy," *Report on Business Magazine,* January 2000: 70–71.

Buchan, James. *Frozen Desire: The Meaning of Money.* New York: Farrar Straus & Giroux, 1997.

"Charity Begins on the Homepage," *Globe and Mail,* 31 May 2000.

"CPP Collapse Seems Likely," *National Post,* 1 February 2000, D4.

Frank, Robert H. *Luxury Fever: Why Money Fails to Satisfy in an Era of Excess.* New York: Free Press, 1999.

Frank, Robert H., and Philip J. Cook. *The Winner-Take-All Society.* Toronto: Penguin, 1996.

French, Serena. "Death by shopping," *National Post,* 10 May 2000, B1.

Galbraith, John Kenneth. *The Affluent Society.* London: Deutsch, 1958.

"In Greed We Trust," *The Economist,* 1 November 1997: 27.

Keynes, John Maynard. *Essays in Persuasion.* New York: Norton, 1963.

Linder, Staffan Burenstam. *The Harried Leisure Class.* New York: Columbia University Press, 1970.

Myers, David G., and Ed Deiner. "Who Is Happy?" *Psychological Science* 6.1 (1995): 10–19.

Needleman, Jacob. *Money and the Meaning of Life.* New York: Currency Doubleday, 1991.

"Not Here: Canada's Final Answer to Quiz-Show Mania," *Globe and Mail,* 21 March 2000.

"Rich Get Richer as Wage Gap Widens," *The Toronto Star,* 22 October 1998.

Samuelson, Robert J. *The Good Life and Its Discontents: The American Dream in the Age of Entitlement.* New York: Random House, 1997.

Stackhouse, John. "The Panhandler's El Dorado," *Globe and Mail,* 20 December 1999, A16.

—. "I'm Tired of Being a Slave to the Church Floor," *Globe and Mail,* 21 December 1999, A16.

Stanley, Alessandra. "Pope Calls on Catholics to Right Church's Wrongs," *Winnipeg Free Press,* 26 December 1999, A18.

Underwood, Nora. "The High Life," *Report on Business Magazine,* January 2000: 67.

Valpy, Michael. "Vatican Issues List of Short Cuts to Heaven," *Globe and Mail,* 18 September 1999, A1.

Veblen, Thorstein. *The Theory of the Leisure Class.* New Brunswick, New Jersey: Transaction Publishers, 1992.

Whyte, William Hollingsworth. *The Organization Man.* Garden City, New York: Doubleday, 1956.